LAWYERS IN POLITICS

AN ADVANCED STUDY IN POLITICAL SCIENCE

Lawyers in Politics

A STUDY IN PROFESSIONAL CONVERGENCE

HEINZ EULAU
Stanford University

and

JOHN D. SPRAGUE
Washington University

THE **BOBBS-MERRILL** COMPANY, INC.
A SUBSIDIARY OF HOWARD W. SAMS & CO., INC.
Publishers • INDIANAPOLIS • NEW YORK

82332

Robert C. Wood
CONSULTING EDITOR
Massachusetts Institute of Technology

TO
OUR FRIENDS AND COLLEAGUES
AT STANFORD UNIVERSITY

PREFACE

This study of lawyers as politicians is a by-product of a much larger project dealing with the political roles and behavior of American state legislators. The data on which it is based were collected in 1957 by the State Legislative Research Project, sponsored by the Political Behavior Committee of the Social Science Research Council and conducted by Professors John C. Wahlke of Vanderbilt University, William Buchanan, then at the University of Southern California and now at the University of Tennessee, LeRoy C. Ferguson of Michigan State University, and the senior author of this monograph. For a full report on the project, the reader may consult *The Legislative System: Explorations in Legislative Behavior* (New York: John Wiley and Sons, 1962). We wish to thank the State Legislative Research Project for permission to use some of its data in this study.

The authors of *The Legislative System* did not attend to the problem of the lawyer in politics even though, in each of the four states of the project, lawyers constituted a significant occupational group in the legislature. Although our analyses make use of the analytical categories developed in connection with *The Legislative System*, this monograph in no way duplicates the main study. Of course, the other authors of the original project are in no way responsible for what we have written.

Apart from primarily enumerative reports or broadly institutional studies, only two political scientists, Professors David R. Derge of Indiana University and Joseph A. Schlesinger of Michigan State University, have dealt systematically with the lawyer's political role—the former in studies of state legislators; the latter, in a study of state governors. In preparing this monograph, we have sought to build on their work, as well as on the work of others who have dealt more incidentally with the lawyer in politics—notably, Leon D. Epstein of the University of Wisconsin, Charles S. Hyneman of Indiana University, and Donald R. Matthews of the University of

North Carolina. We have greatly benefited also from several more theoretical writings about the legal profession, especially essays by Robert E. Agger of the University of Oregon, Talcott Parsons, and David Riesman. Our starting points were the classical statements about lawyers in politics by Alexis de Tocqueville, James Bryce, and Max Weber. The work of the legal historian James Willard Hurst provided much-needed background. We wish to acknowledge here our indebtedness to all those whose contributions, large or small, theoretical or empirical, make a cumulative science of politics possible.

Before preparing the final version of this monograph, we had the benefit of careful criticism and useful comment from the following friends and colleagues: Robert E. Agger, University of Oregon; William Buchanan, University of Tennessee; Richard Fagen, Stanford University; Robert Peabody, The Johns Hopkins University; Howard Sachs, Northwestern University Law School; Martin Shapiro, Stanford University; Joseph A. Schlesinger, Michigan State University; John C. Wahlke, Vanderbilt University; and Everett K. Wilson, Antioch College. These gentlemen saved us from many errors of omission and commission; for any errors that may remain, we take sole responsibility.

HEINZ EULAU

JOHN D. SPRAGUE

Stanford University
March 1, 1964

CONTENTS

LIST OF TABLES

The profession I chose was politics;
the profession I entered was the law.
I entered one because I thought
it would lead to the other.

Woodrow Wilson

INTRODUCTION

A persistent question of inquiry is always to justify one's "problem" as being worth the time and effort required to study it systematically. When we began to look at the data on lawyer-legislators in four American states, we took it for granted that the lawyer's prominence in politics was "problematical," though we were not quite certain just what the "problem" was. But had the affinity of law and politics not fascinated some of the most distinguished observers of political institutions, from Alexis de Tocqueville, James Bryce, and Max Weber to such contemporaries as Talcott Parsons and David Riesman? Our initial idea, certainly, was to see whether the data we had could throw light on, if not test, some of the propositions about lawyers in politics that are to be found in the literature. But we soon realized that the classical observations could not serve our research needs. For we discovered an empirical paradox that required a fresh theoretical departure. It is this paradox that became our "problem."

The paradox is essentially this: Though lawyers are clearly a distinct occupational group that is more visible, more ubiquitous, more prominent, and even more dominant in American political life than in any other, their private profession does not seem to affect a great deal of their political behavior. To put this somewhat differently, though he is a lawyer, the lawyer-politician does not differ appreciably from other politicians. Our problem became one of explaining the lack of differences between lawyers and nonlawyers in politics—not by discounting private occupation as an explanatory factor, but by continuing to use it as a major element in a theoretical schema.

The organization of this monograph reflects, therefore, the "natural history" of our research. We began our work by examining some of the apprehensions widely entertained about the consequences of the lawyer's ubiquity in the political process. We shall present this and other "background" material in Chapter 1. The topics treated in Chapters 2 to 4 were largely "given" by the data that were available

3

to us from the larger project on state legislators. This limited what we could and could not do, in regard both to the populations we studied and to the variables we used in the analyses. And, though we relied on whatever speculative "handles" we could find in the traditional literature on lawyers in politics, these analyses were not formulated in terms of the theoretical considerations presented in Chapter 5. These theoretical efforts did not precede our inspection of the data but followed it.

If it is inappropriate for us to claim that we were guided by an explicit theory in looking at the data, however, it would be unjust to deny us any kind of theoretical concern as we approached the data. We had some quite definite, if poorly articulated, notions that the affinity of law and politics might be accounted for by some functional equivalence of the lawyer's role in the legal system and the politician's role in the political system. But we assumed this to be a working hypothesis rather than a hypothesis that could be verified or negated with the material at hand. We therefore resisted the temptation to introduce what theoretical notions we came up with after analyzing the data as if they had given us research direction all along.

Post-factum theorizing of this sort is, admittedly, the price one pays for "secondary analysis" of data not collected for the immediate research objective at hand. But it seems to us that using such data is preferable to using no data whatever. Ideally, of course, a research design for a study of lawyers in politics would want to provide for three groups: first, a randomly selected group of lawyer-politicians; second, a randomly selected group of lawyers who are not politicians; and third, a similarly selected group of politicians who are not lawyers. Only comparison of the "experimental" lawyer-politician group with both "control groups" could justify reliable inferences about lawyers in politics that are more than tentative. A study of this kind is not beyond the reach of the methodological imagination, but we must settle for a simpler design.

This study involves comparison only of lawyer-politicians and nonlawyer-politicians, or, more accurately, of lawyer-legislators and nonlawyer-legislators in four American states. Though legislators can be called "politicians" (but some might disavow the label), not all politicians are legislators. If, at times, we speak of politicians when it would be more correct to speak of legislators, it is for the simple reason of breaking the monotony of one usage. We do not assume that what we say about politicians who are legislators is in any way representative or typical of all politicians—and neither is it representative of all legislators.

Comparison of lawyer- and nonlawyer-legislators may allow us to make inferences concerning these groups, then, but it does not tell us anything about what may be even more interesting—namely, what one might be able to say about lawyer-politicians as compared with lawyers who are not in politics. On the other hand, such comparisons as we make in this study can serve a purpose that is of particular interest to political science. As political scientists, we are primarily concerned not with the sociology of a profession, even one as close to politics as is law, but with the consequences of a professional group's presence for the functioning of a political system. As we are concerned with the legal profession's impact on the functioning of a governmental institution—the legislature—comparison of lawyer- and nonlawyer-legislators alone seems to constitute a sufficiently appropriate research design. For lawyers who are not members of the institution do not directly influence its functioning (though they might do so in political roles that are not legislative—as lobbyists, expert witnesses, private citizens, and so on).

The basic design of this study is, therefore, a very simple one. Legislators were distinguished as lawyers and nonlawyers by their declared occupation. Analytical attention is focused primarily on similarities or differences in the distributions of the two groups on whatever measures are used to examine their responses to interview questions about their perceptions, attitudes, orientations, behavior, and so on. However, as we are dealing with four different legislative systems, the patterns of distribution across states are of equal interest. Such interstate patterns, as we suggest in the Appendix, are significant bases of inference concerning whatever distributions may be found in a single system. In the Appendix, too, we include the interview questions from which our data derive as well as the typologies and scales that were constructed to make the data analytically manageable. We also discuss there some of the statistical problems involved in this kind of analysis and suggest the utility of comparison as a method of inference.

This is a study of two professions that, we shall argue, are "convergent." What do we mean by "profession"? A profession consists of a set of more or less well institutionalized requirements that its practitioners are expected to meet. Within the larger institutional structure of society, a profession is very similar to "status" positions in an organization. Like positions in an organizational hierarchy, professions are evaluated in terms of the status they confer on their practitioners. And, like positions, professions are critical connective structures between the individual and the larger society. If we know a man's profession, we know his "place" in the social order. Positions or professions, then, are never unique to a particular individual; they are invariably "historic" in character in that particular individuals can follow each other in time in occupying a position (hence "occupation") or in pursuing a profession. The pursuit of an occupation or profession constitutes a person's "career." The career begins with appropriate training and recruitment, and it is fulfilled as skills are applied in the performance of the tasks for which, presumably, the occupation or profession has come into existence in the first place. Because these tasks may be manifold, involving interactions with a variety of others, they give rise to roles that are taken in their performance. Just as a man's job, occupation, or profession links him as an individual with the social structure, so his career is likely to be a critical nexus linking occupation or profession with the roles that arise in the performance of vocational tasks. An objective of research, then, is to identify particular career patterns with particular roles.[1]

Although careers in Western society are generally thought of in terms of specific occupations or jobs, it is possible, as Everett C.

[1] See William Form and Delbert C. Miller, "Occupational Career Pattern as a Sociological Instrument," *American Journal of Sociology*, LIV (January 1949), 317–329.

Hughes has observed, "to have a career in an avocation as well as in a vocation."[2] This observation is particularly relevant in the case of politics because, as we shall argue, though politics *tends to meet* the criteria of professionalism, it is underdeveloped in comparison with other professions, and especially that of the law. It may sound paradoxical to speak of a "professional politician" who practices politics as an avocation, just as it may sound paradoxical to speak of an "amateur politician" for whom politics is a vocation—in its literal sense a "calling" which, for whatever reason, he cannot resist. But, as terms often are in the social sciences, such terms as "professional" or "amateur" are ambiguous and unstable in usage. Each investigator is, of course, free to define his working concepts as he wishes, as long as he applies them consistently in his own work.[3]

Whether a lawyer perceives his pursuit of politics as a second vocation or as a hobby is, of course, always a matter of empirical determination. But in the case of the lawyer, his profession as a lawyer seems to be particularly effective in defining his "extra-professional" role as a politician. By "extra-professional" role we mean those expectations and obligations that are based on the lawyer's professional role but that do not arise directly from his professional relationships. The lawyer evidently is expected to do political things that are not part of his functions as a lawyer but are expected of him simply because he is a lawyer. As two sociologists put it in a study concerned with the lawyer's "extra-professional" role, his political role

> . . . is in the penumbra of the professional role, so to speak. We may define it residually as those behavior expectations pertaining

---

[2] Everett C. Hughes, "Institutional Office and The Person," in *Men and Their Work* (Glencoe: The Free Press, 1958), p. 64.

[3] See, for instance, the partly similar, partly different formulation by James Q. Wilson, who defines the amateur as "one who finds politics *intrinsically* interesting because it expresses a conception of the public interest. The amateur politician sees the political world more in terms of ideas and principles than in terms of persons." The professional, "even the 'professional' who practices politics as a hobby rather than as a vocation—is preoccupied with the outcome of politics in terms of winning or losing." *The Amateur Democrat: Club Politics in Three Cities* (Chicago: University of Chicago Press, 1962), pp. 3–4.

to the lawyer in relation to his community and society which are not those of every citizen and which are not part of the technical function of the lawyer.[4]

If the lawyer's political role is "in the penumbra of the professional role," his political career is, indeed, the crucial link between his professional role as a lawyer and his role as a politician, regardless whether he conceives of it as vocation or as avocation. We would think that his career in politics—the circumstances of his political socialization, the opportunities accompanying his entry into active politics, and the conditions that facilitate or impede his political mobility—will be decisive in determining whether, in due course, he becomes a professional politician or remains a devoted amateur. Needless to say, professional status in politics is forever closed to many lawyers and nonlawyers alike because there are only a limited number of positions to be filled. But if, as Hughes put it, "a career is the moving perspective in which the person sees his life as a whole and interprets the meaning of his various attributes, actions, and the things which happen to him,"[5] it links the lawyer-politician's position in the institutional structure of society and the particular roles that he may take in the pursuit of politics. For, as Hughes continues, "this perspective is not absolutely fixed either as to points of view, direction, or destination."[6]

POLITICAL ROLES AS UNITS OF INQUIRY

Although a profession functions within the human division of labor as a relatively unified group of experts who bring to the solution of societal problems a particular body of technical or scientific knowledge, a man's profession no longer tells us very much about just what he does or is expected to do. In both law and politics,

---

[4] Walter I. Wardwell and Arthur L. Wood, "The Extra-Professional Role of the Lawyer," *American Journal of Sociology*, LXI (January 1956), 304.

[5] Hughes, *op. cit.*, p. 63.

[6] *Ibid.*

internal specialization has gone far. For this reason, focusing research on the entire profession as the unit of inquiry does not carry analysis very far. For instance, breaking up the lawyer's role into "professional" and "extra-professional" roles can serve only as a first step; it does not exhaust the possibilities. Similarly, the conventional distinction of public officials as judges, legislators, or administrators, whatever uses it may have in institutional analysis, does not tell us very much about what is expected of incumbents of judicial, legislative, or administrative positions. If the affinity of law and politics is to be explained in terms of "professional convergence," more discriminating differentiation of the roles taken by lawyers in their "legal" work and by politicians in their "political" work is called for. Convergence should be more easily observable on the microscopic level of roles than on the macroscopic level of professions.

But why inquire into the diverse roles taken by lawyers or politicians in the division of functions rather than into the functions themselves? We may draw again on the wisdom of Everett C. Hughes. He writes,

> The division of labor, in its turn, implies interaction; for it consists not in the sheer difference of one man's kind of work from that of another, but in the fact that the different tasks and accomplishments are parts of a whole to whose product all, in some degree, contribute. And wholes, in the human social realm as in the rest of the biological and in the physical realm, have their essence in interaction.[7]

Role is a concept that has been given a great variety of nominal and operational meanings—for theoretical reasons that are equally numerous. These differences in usage are not our concern here.[8] It is sufficient to say that role is a concept, generic to all the social

[7] Everett C. Hughes, "Social Role and the Division of Labor," *op. cit.*, p. 68.

[8] The literature on role is legion. For convenient summaries, see especially Theodore R. Sarbin, "Role Theory," in Gardner Lindzey (ed.), *Handbook of Social Psychology* (Reading, Mass.: Addison-Wesley Publishing Company, 1954), I, 235–258; and Neal Gross, Ward S. Mason, and Alexander W. McEachern, *Explorations in Role Analysis* (New York: John Wiley & Sons, 1958), pp. 3–75.

sciences, that permits a multilevel attack on man's interpersonal relations as well as on his institutional connections.[9] On the level of political analysis, roles may be conceived as providing the premises in terms of which political actors relate themselves to each other, to their clients, and to the decision-making situations in which they find themselves.[10] Role is clearly a concept consistent with the analytic objective of behavioral inquiry. It is predicated on the interrelatedness and interdependence of people. For this reason, it seems especially useful in studying professional convergence.

---

[9] For further elaboration, see Heinz Eulau, *The Behavioral Persuasion in Politics* (New York: Random House, 1963).

[10] For an interpretation of role as setting "premises" in decision-making, see Herbert A. Simon, *Models of Man* (New York: John Wiley & Sons, 1957), p. 201.

Chapter 1

HIGH PRIESTS OF POLITICS

No occupational group stands in more regular and intimate relation to American politics than the legal profession. Lawyers make up a large proportion of American politicians at all levels and in all branches of government, in the political parties, and in other political organizations. The affinity of law and politics as vocations is a matter of record. In the United States, probably more than in any other nation, lawyers are the "high priests of politics." The legal profession provides the most substantial reservoir of political personnel.

That lawyers have an almost complete monopoly of public offices connected with law enforcement and with the administration of law in the courts is not surprising. But they are also prominent as an occupational group in the executive and legislative arenas of government. This has been true from the earliest days of the republic. Of the fifty-two signers of the Declaration of Independence, twenty-five were lawyers, as were thirty-one of the fifty-five members serving in the Continental Congress. Of the thirty-six American presidents, twenty-three have been lawyers.[1] Between 1877 and 1934, 70 per cent of American presidents, vice-presidents, and cabinet members were lawyers.[2] Of a total of 995 elected governors in all American

---

[1] Donald R. Matthews, *The Social Background of Political Decision-Makers* (Garden City, N.Y.: Doubleday & Company, 1954), p. 30.

[2] H. Dewey Anderson, "The Educational and Occupational Attainments of Our National Rulers," *Scientific Monthly*, XL (June 1935), 511–518.

states between 1870 and 1950, 46 per cent were practicing lawyers.[3]

In the legislative branches, the ascendancy of the legal profession is equally marked. Of 175 members serving in the Senate of the United States between 1947 and 1957, 54 per cent were lawyers.[4] In the seventy-first through the seventy-fifth Congresses, from 61 to 76 per cent of the members of the Senate and from 56 to 65 per cent of the members of the House of Representatives belonged to the legal profession.[5] Between 1925 and 1935, of a total of 12,689 persons serving in the lower houses of thirteen selected states and in the upper houses of twelve, 28 per cent were lawyers by occupation.[6] A survey of all 7,475 American state legislators serving in 1949 showed that 22 per cent were lawyers.[7] About 30 per cent of the members of the Wisconsin legislature in 1957 were attorneys,[8] as were 25 per cent of those serving in the Indiana General Assembly in 1959.[9] In the four legislatures of New Jersey, Ohio, Tennessee, and California in 1957—where the data for the present study were collected—52, 36, 30, and 30 per cent of the members, respectively, were lawyers.

---

[3] Joseph A. Schlesinger, "Lawyers and American Politics: A Clarified View," *Midwest Journal of Political Science*, I (May 1957), 28. Not included in the proportion of lawyers here are those who have been admitted to the bar or who hold law degrees but do not practice law.

[4] Donald R. Matthews, *U.S. Senators and Their World* (Chapel Hill: University of North Carolina Press, 1960), pp. 33–36.

[5] John Brown Mason, "Lawyers in the 71st to 75th Congress: Their Legal Education and Experience," *Rocky Mountain Law Review*, X (December 1937), 44.

[6] Charles S. Hyneman, "Who Makes Our Laws?" in John C. Wahlke and Heinz Eulau, *Legislative Behavior* (Glencoe: The Free Press, 1959), p. 255, Table 1. The article was first published in *Political Science Quarterly*, LV (December 1940), 556–581.

[7] Belle Zeller (ed.), *American State Legislatures* (New York: Thomas Y. Crowell, 1954), p. 71, Table 4.

[8] Leon D. Epstein, *Politics in Wisconsin* (Madison: University of Wisconsin Press, 1958), p. 188, Table VI-A.

[9] David R. Derge, "The Lawyer in the Indiana General Assembly," *Midwest Journal of Political Science*, VI (February 1962), 21.

There is no need to belabor further the fact of the lawyer's ubiquity in politics. It is surely an outstanding phenomenon of American political life. But, lest the political aspect be given undue emphasis, the lawyer's role in the economy deserves at least incidental mention. Just as lawyers were critically influential in building the American polity and remain so in guiding it, they were equally influential in shaping the American economy, and they continue to be so. Not accidentally, perhaps, the legal profession grew most conspicuously with the rapid growth of commerce, finance, and industry in the decades around the transition from the nineteenth century to the twentieth. Law was "one of the careers through which a man could attain influence and wealth even without having capital at the start; and the fortunes accumulated by a few men at the bar were taken as an index of its normal possibilities."[10] Lawyers not only serve all kinds of economic enterprise in one professional capacity or another, but they also sit as influential members on the boards of banks, railroads, manufacturing concerns, and educational institutions. Quite apart from the economy's functional needs for the lawyer's skills, it is plausible that, in a business civilization such as that of the United States, lawyers should seek fame or fortune by associating themselves with commerce and industry.

By way of contrast, the lawyer's visibility in politics represents a paradox. One side of this paradox stems from traditional criticisms of the legal profession; the other side, from the low popular estimate of politics as a career. The American bar, states the report on the Survey of the Legal Profession conducted in the late forties and early fifties, has been criticized "in such characterizations as 'lawyers are financially dishonest,' 'lawyers are liars,' 'lawyers are tools of big business,' and 'lawyers have too much power.' "[11] This side of the

---

[10] William Miller, "American Lawyers in Business and in Politics: Their Social Backgrounds and Early Training," *Yale Law Journal*, LX (January 1951), 73.

[11] Albert P. Blaustein and Charles O. Porter, *The American Lawyer: A Summary of the Survey of the Legal Profession* (Chicago: University of Chicago Press, 1954), p. 35. For discussion of criticisms, see especially pp. 32–37 and 254–263.

paradox, as Professor Harry W. Jones of the Columbia University Law School put it, is that "the public is often severely critical of lawyers *as lawyers*, but it has a marked preference for them as public officials."[12]

The second side of the paradox is reflected in the results of a public opinion poll conducted in November 1945 by the National Opinion Research Center. A cross section of the American people was asked this question: "If you had a son just getting out of school, would you like to see him go into politics as a lifework?" Respondents were asked also whether they would like their son to "become a lawyer." The results:[13]

	YES	NO	NO OPINION DON'T KNOW	QUALIFIED ANSWER	TOTAL
Politics	24%	65%	10%	1%	100%
Law	62%	26%	11%	1%	100%

In view of the close relationship between law and politics as vocations, the conspicuous contrast in public attitudes expressed by these figures is astounding. If law be a desirable profession, and if lawyers make desirable candidates for political office, the low esteem in which politics evidently is held as a vocation would seem to betray an almost schizophrenic perception of public life. Whatever the psychological explanation, that so many would like to see their sons become lawyers and yet so few would like to see them go into politics as their lifework suggests that the affinity of law and politics as vocations is more ambiguous than one might at first suspect.

The conventional explanation of the lawyer's dominance in politics is, as Alexis de Tocqueville put it long ago, that "scarcely any question arises in the United States which does not become, sooner or later, a subject of judicial debate."[14] In contrast to the

---

[12] Quoted in *ibid.*, p. 99.

[13] Hadley Cantril and Mildred Strunk, *Public Opinion, 1935–46* (Princeton: Princeton University Press, 1951), p. 534.

[14] Alexis de Tocqueville, *Democracy in America,* translated by Henry Reeve (New York: Oxford University Press, 1947), p. 177. This work was first published in France, in two parts, in 1835 and 1840.

mother country, where the final locus of political power, as the outcome of the struggle between Crown and Parliament, was acknowledged in the latter's legal sovereignty, in the United States the political power of the legislature was inhibited by constitutional limitations. But if the power of the legislature is limited, who is in a better position than the lawyer to know whether the Constitution has been violated? In view of the passion for lawmaking that prevailed among a people which confidently believed that the solution of all problems could be found in the enactment of statutes, the veneration of the Constitution seemed all the more necessary. No wonder, also, that in the course of the great conflicts between the judiciary and the other branches of government, not only did the judiciary come to assume for itself guardianship of the Constitution, but also, in the United States alone among Western nations, the courts often emerged as the ultimate arbiters of political questions. And as in the higher reaches of the American polity the Constitution became the sacred symbol of judicial over executive or legislative supremacy, in the lower reaches the courthouse became the symbol not only of the country's legal but also of its political culture. The "courthouse gang" became the prototype of the urban political machine. The lawyer was on his way to political dominance.

The prominence of the legal profession in politics, then, is traditionally attributed to the American reverence for law—to the tendency to substitute legal for political considerations in the formulation of public policies and to judge political results by legal standards. This traditional explanation has some aspects that commend it— lawyers do play an important role in politics as legal technicians. It is an explanation that lawyer-politicians may themselves give for their presence in politics. In our study of lawyer-legislators in four states, some respondents gave answers such as the following to the question concerning the manner in which they became members of the legislature:

> When I served on the probate bench, I was president of the Association of Probate Judges, the Association of Juvenile Court Judges, and secretary of the National Council of Juvenile Court

Judges. While I held these offices, I was often required to appear before legislative committees to testify as to the legality of certain bills. That experience caused me to become interested in the legislature, and I decided that I would rather make up the bills than have to come in afterwards to decide if it was legal.

Being an attorney and having training in and being naturally interested in laws, well, deriving from that, I had an active interest in the making of laws.

As these and other comments made in the interview protocols suggest, lawmaking is seen by some as a legal activity rather than as a political one. But it is by no means clear just what is cause and what is effect in this explanation. Did public reverence for law and Constitution precede the political ascendancy of the lawyer, or did it spring from the lawyer's prominence in politics? The question is one for historians to decide. As a functional hypothesis for explaining the affinity between law and politics as vocations, the conventional approach seems highly inadequate.

The mere fact that lawyers are highly visible in politics is not by itself proof that their presence makes a difference in the functioning of political institutions. But many observers have certainly believed that it does. A convenient starting point for this investigation, therefore, is the various types and expressions of concern about the legal profession's prominent place in politics that have been voiced by some of these observers.

By way of background, it is well to recall that, in the formative years of the country, lawyers were considered particularly suited for careers in government. Like clergymen and medical men, they were accorded social recognition and prestige not because they were men of power or wealth (though they might be), but because their vocation was seen as one of public service and public trust. "In the profession's golden age of public leadership—the years from 1765 to 1830," writes the legal historian James Willard Hurst, "we find qualities of independence of judgment, and pride in the responsibility and dignity of legal counseling and the shaping of social institutions, such as were not manifested with equal vigor later on."[15] A hundred years later, however, a prominent lawyer complained that "Intellectually the profession commanded and still commands respect, but it is the respect for an intellectual jobber and contractor rather than for a moral force."[16] On the level of rhetoric, the problem has been stated as follows:

> If the bar . . . is to state quite honestly the measure of its participation in public life, it must admit that law-trained persons maintain a complete monopoly over one branch of government and considerable effective control over the other two. The fact of numerical ascendancy alone indicates that, to the extent to which government exercises authority over the development and well-being of this nation, the bar is responsible in no small measure for determining the future of the society, and, as a consequence, its own future. From this heavy responsibility, it cannot escape except by relinquishing, or being forced to relinquish, a considerable part of its intervention in public affairs.[17]

This discussion will consider four sources of concern about the lawyer in politics. These are his "over-representation," his potential exploitation of his numerical superiority for selfish purposes, his alleged conservatism, and his deficient training for public policy-making.

APPREHENSION NUMBER ONE: OVER-REPRESENTATION

The interest here is not in the lawyer's responsibility as an expert adviser on legal matters to or as an active policy-maker in the judicial and executive branches of government, but in his role as an elective public official in legislative bodies. In these bodies the

---

[15] James Willard Hurst, *The Growth of American Law: The Law Makers* (Boston: Little, Brown and Company, 1950), p. 366.

[16] A. A. Berle, Jr., "Modern Legal Profession," *Encyclopaedia of the Social Sciences* (New York: The Macmillan Company, 1933), IX, 344.

[17] Esther L. Brown, *Lawyers, Law Schools, and the Public Service* (New York: Russell Sage Foundation, 1948), pp. 20–21.

lawyer's visibility has, time and again, called attention to the alleged "over-representation" of the legal profession compared with other occupations. The question immediately arises whether this is a genuine social problem that deserves public concern and scholarly inquiry. That it is a problem, or is perceived as one, was implicit in a spate of early studies dealing with the occupational composition of legislatures.[18] The dire consequences presumably expected to follow from this over-representation were rarely specified, though it was invariably pointed out that lawyers have always constituted less than one per cent of the United States labor force.

Representation is admittedly a continuing problem of democratic politics. It is a common observation that not all men are equally well equipped to perform the representational function. Granted that only certain men will have the requisite skills, intelligence, or character, does not selective recruitment of representatives violate democratic ideals and introduce a serious bias into the democratic process? American democracy has traditionally placed a high value on equality—or, rather, on "equality of opportunity." Implicit in this value is a consensus concerning what ought to be the bases of social distinctions. Allowable or legitimate distinctions are those that rest on demonstrated ability and achievement.

The authors of *The Federalist* were sensitive to the need for arguing the case for the new Constitution at least partially in these terms. Who is to be elected to the House of Representatives? "Every citizen whose merit may recommend him to the esteem and confidence of his country." Unequivocal as the statement was, it was not left at that; what was *not* required by the Constitution was clearly stated:

> No qualification of wealth, of birth, of religious faith, or of *civil profession* is permitted to fetter the judgment or disappoint the inclination of the people.[19]

---

[18] In addition to studies already cited, see also Madge M. McKinney, "The Personnel of the 77th Congress," *American Political Science Review*, XXXVI (February 1942), 67–75.

[19] Alexander Hamilton, James Madison, and John Jay, *The Federalist, or, The New Constitution*, edited, with an introduction and notes, by Max Beloff (New York: The Macmillan Company, 1948), pp. 292–293. Italics in text have been added.

The last disclaimer—no qualification of civil profession—seems to be belied by the preponderance, in proportional terms, of lawyers in legislative bodies. But direct proportionality of characteristics, and especially of occupational characteristics, of representative and represented, even if it were possible, is not a requisite of the democratic process. Moreover, a question of this kind, though perhaps important from the vantage point of normative political theory, does not lend itself to empirical proof or disproof. It can be demonstrated by any scheme of classification, and it has been demonstrated, that legislatures are not "representative" of the general population in any proportional sense.[20]

Even if it were only radical democrats who bemoaned the over-representation of the legal profession in legislatures or elsewhere, as a matter of political principle, the suspicion would yet remain that lawyers are in some way subverting the will of the people—in short, that the over-representation of lawyers as a group affects policy outcomes in ways that would not occur if fewer lawyers were active in politics. The question was raised, but not answered, in an article that was typical of the earlier writings on lawyers as legislators:

> On an opinion basis there are two points of view about lawyers: (1) that they are villains, that they dominate the legislatures, represent big vested interests, follow precedent, and stand in the way of progress; (2) that they are public benefactors, a constructive force in our legislatures, and represent varied and conflicting interests, whereby a solution of problems is reached conducive to progress and the public welfare.[21]

Whatever evidence there may be for either one of these consequences of the lawyers' presence in politics, their over-representation, so called, is not a genuine political problem if it is formulated in these terms, nor does it constitute a particularly challenging question for research.

---

[20] Harold F. Gosnell, *Democracy—The Threshold of Freedom* (New York: The Ronald Press Company, 1948), pp. 224–232.

[21] M. Louise Rutherford, "Lawyers as Legislators," *The Annals of the American Academy of Political and Social Science*, CXCV (January 1938), 53.

APPREHENSION NUMBER TWO: A CONSPIRACY

Implicit in the concern about the over-representation of lawyers in legislative bodies is the apprehension that they do, can, or will form a cohesive bloc that can, does, or will unfairly use its numerical strength to seek legislation favorable to the interest of the legal profession. Sometimes this apprehension is made explicit, as in a statement by the late Governor Herbert Lehman of New York, who is reported to have complained of "the conspiracy of lawyer-legislators to perpetrate for their profession the obstructions to justice by which it prospers."[22]

What is the evidence? In his study of American interest groups, David B. Truman noted that "the centrifugal effects of specialized practice and wide income differentials have placed limits on the effectiveness with which bar associations stabilize the relationships of their potential membership and upon the completeness of association among lawyers."[23] If lawyers are not united *outside* the legislature, why should one expect them to be united *inside* it? The only careful and detailed studies of this problem have been made by David R. Derge in Illinois, Indiana, and Missouri. In his first study, one of the Illinois and Missouri lower houses in 1955 and 1957, Derge selected a sample of contested roll calls in order to analyze the voting cohesions of lawyers, farmers, and a control group selected at random without regard to occupation (though the control group included the same proportions of Democrats and Republicans as did the lawyer group). Derge found that the lawyers did not regularly vote together with high cohesion. In his own words:

> As the level of cohesion increased the frequency of lawyer solidarity decreased until in no instance did lawyers vote with a cohesion

---

[22] Quoted in Robert S. Allen, *Our Sovereign State* (New York: Vanguard, 1949), p. xxxvii.

[23] David B. Truman, *The Governmental Process* (New York: Alfred A. Knopf, 1951), p. 96.

of 90% or more on at least 1% of the session's roll-calls. . . . Perhaps the most telling commentary on lawyer solidarity is that the cohesion patterns of the control groups closely resemble those of the lawyers. On the whole lawyers voted less often with high cohesion than did the control group, which suggests that there is no more reason to expect lawyers to act with unity than to expect a group of legislators chosen at random to vote together. If there were a solid lawyer "bloc" or "cell" in decision-making the frequency of high cohesion would be much greater.[24]

Derge found also that, if cohesion among lawyers is related to the degree of conflict on roll calls, "as the degree of controversy on policy increases, high lawyer cohesion, which is infrequent at best, decreases until it disappears when the chamber is fairly evenly divided."[25] Moreover, high lawyer cohesion, when it occurred, was not characteristic of any particular type of bill. In view of this, and because lawyer solidarity probably resulted from chance, Derge concludes that "lawyers reacted to public policy decisions on some other basis than professional identification."[26]

In a second study, of the 1949 and 1957 sessions of the Indiana General Assembly, Derge produced even stronger evidence in examining the voting behavior of lawyers on roll calls directly affecting their profession—six on bills relating to the fee structure for legal services in various areas of civil practice, and nine on bills concerning the structure and organization of the judicial system. On all but one of these roll calls, the lawyers divided in approximately the same way as the nonlawyers did. Derge concludes that "there is no 'lawyer bloc' in roll-calls involving public policy intimately related to the practice of the law."[27]

Whether this kind of evidence would convince those who believe that lawyers have a pernicious influence on legislative affairs cannot

---

[24] David R. Derge, "The Lawyer as Decision-Maker in the American State Legislature," *Journal of Politics*, XXI (August 1959), 427.

[25] *Ibid.*, p. 428.

[26] *Ibid.*, p. 429.

[27] Derge, "The Lawyer in the Indiana General Assembly," *op. cit.*, p. 49.

be known. Some comments made in the course of interviews with nonlawyer-legislators in four state legislatures may serve to illustrate the antagonism shown toward lawyers by some of their lay colleagues:

> There are too many lawyers. They represent clients, try to win lawsuits in the legislature that they can't win in the courts.

> Lawyers draw up laws so nobody including themselves can understand them. It makes business for them. Judges have to decide in courts what laws mean and sometimes they reverse themselves. Laws could be drafted that would be clear and simple if they wanted to.

> Lawyers are lousy legislators because they have too much technical attitude. They can't look at it as laymen can. They can't see practical problems. They are too much interested in legal technicalities. The lawyer is good to defend you or give you legal advice, he's not good to represent all the people. The average layman is better equipped to be a legislator.

> We shouldn't ever send an attorney to the legislature. They get so many laws to suit their own individual jobs that a wayfarin' man can't understand.

None of these hostile observations accuses the lawyers of conspiratorial cooperation among themselves; and, while the lawyer's technical know-how serves as the immediate target of criticism, there are other complaints—"win lawsuits," "makes business," "not good to represent all the people," "laws to suit their own individual jobs." Unfortunately, present data do not tell us how widely shared these negative attitudes of nonlawyers toward lawyers in the legislatures are, or to what extent these attitudes "define the situation" in lawyer–nonlawyer relationships in legislative work.

APPREHENSION NUMBER THREE: CONSERVATISM

Even if lawyers do not constitute cohesive, solidary voting blocs in legislatures, it is alleged that as individuals they are "conservatives," and that their numerical superiority serves through this trait to give

one-sided direction to public policies. The arguments about the
lawyer's conservatism are often persuasive but are usually based
on slim evidence. They seem to involve three points. First, the lawyer
is conservative because the ways of the law are "by nature" conservative. Second, he is conservative because the institutional matrix
of the legal system makes him so. And third, he is conservative because he is invariably tied to economic interests that are conservative. All these statements are inferences about attitudes or behavior
made from rather global considerations. Although the inferences
are more or less valid on the surface, they are rarely tested in the
crucible of empirical research.

The first argument has been stated well by the late Harold J.
Laski:

> It is almost an inevitable characteristic of the legal mind that
> it should tend to conservatism. It is largely engaged in the study
> of precedent. What it can do is most often set by the statutes of a
> preceding generation. Its chief exponents are, as a rule, men already
> well past middle age who come to positions of authority just when
> new wants they have not known are coming to be expressed.
> Lawyers, in fact, are more definitely the servants of tradition, than
> any other class in the community; for the demonstration that novelty
> is desirable is, with them, more difficult, because more impalpable,
> than with any other aspect of social life.[28]

It would be foolish to deny that a person's political perspective
is conditioned crucially by his occupational experiences. Most men
spend the better part of their working day in the company of colleagues. Under these conditions and given similar training, lawyers,
like other professionals, are likely to come to share certain attitudes
of mind. The case approach, the search for precedent, and suspicion
of doctrinal purity are probably part of every Anglo-American
lawyer's mental baggage. But this does not, *ipso facto*, make lawyers
conservative in the political sense of the term. To say that lawyers

---

[28] Harold J. Laski, *A Grammar of Politics* (New Haven: Yale University Press,
1929), p. 572.

are politically conservative because the methods of the legal process are conservative is, if not semantic nonsense, at best evidence
for the fallacy of "affirming the consequent." Law, it is true, seeks
regularity and predictability of human affairs, but it can be employed also as an instrument of social change. Because it can be
used for ends that are "conservative" or "liberal," whatever these
terms may mean at any time, the validity of inferences from its
methods to the political attitudes of its practitioners seems highly
dubious.

Second, it is alleged that, although law may be an instrument of
either standpattism or change, the method of recruitment to the
much-coveted positions of the American judiciary is such that conservatism among lawyers is favored. Rather than being trained directly for a judicial career, as judges are in Europe, American judges
are elected or appointed to the bench only after they have gained
reputations at the bar. This means, the argument continues, that
judges are relatively old; and age makes for conservatism. And
because the judge is the lawyer's ego-ideal, and because the lawyer
must practice before judges, the lawyer tends to develop conservative attitudes that may aid him in climbing the judicial ladder.

It is certainly true that in several periods of American judicial
history, and notably in the history of the Supreme Court, some
judges were archconservatives in the political sense of the term.
With great ingenuity they invented the fiction of liberty of contract
to strike down legislation designed to improve the hours, wages, and
conditions of workingmen; they discovered in the Fourteenth
Amendment, and especially in its due process clause, a protection of
the right of giant corporations; and they denied, in the name of the
Constitution, almost all social welfare legislation—from the federal
income tax to the numerous measures of the New Deal. But whether
this behavior was due to their age, and whether aspiring young
lawyers pattern their own political vision in the image of the "old
men," is a matter of derivative speculation not much sounder than
the argument that identifies conservatism with the "legal mind."
And the argument fails to account for the not-very-rare liberal
dissenters on the bench.

A third argument has it that the lawyer is conservative because, all other factors being equal, he receives the bulk of his business from those who can afford his services; and those who can afford them best are the powerful and conservative interests of financial and industrial wealth. The argument may be valid in the case of some lawyers, perhaps even of many lawyers, but supportive evidence is meager. Just as the "average lawyer" cannot be assumed to be a photocopy of the conservative judge, neither can he be assumed to be a replica of the "corporation lawyer," whose image is likely to be conservative. One cannot simply ignore the facts that few lawyers are wealthy (though some are very wealthy) and that even fewer work as corporation lawyers. Moreover, lawyers have served not only corporate interests; they have served labor unions and humanitarian groups as well. And they have been in the forefront of liberal reform.

Until a fair inventory of the legal profession's ideological orientations has been made, the argument about the lawyer's conservatism, based on his presumed relationship to the economic powers bent on maintaining the status quo, is no less a hazardous inference from unsubstantiated assumptions than the other arguments that have been reviewed. Taking the long view, the historian Hurst writes:

> From the vantage of 1950—in a country newly conscious of how sensitively interrelated were men's interests and institutions—it might appear that for one hundred years past the bar had not fulfilled the constructive role open to it; it might appear that lawyers had been too preoccupied with law as a game, or as instruments for private ends. If an observer were measurably justified in passing this judgment, he was not thereby entitled to any moral complacency. Lawyers had shared the going values and vision of their times. With other people in the United States, they had joined in economic and social growth that was daring and constructive, and also in growth that was ruthless and wasteful. With others they had—after the creative generation that produced the Constitution—been indifferent, hostile, or timid toward adapting their political institutions to the sweep of change. As a group or organized guild, lawyers had stood inert or antagonistic before some imperative needs to reform law and its administration. Nonetheless, individual lawyers were counted among the initiators, architects,

and administrators of much of the constructive work in social control after the '70s. Many of the counts that might be leveled against the bar must in justice be directed equally at the society which it reflected.[29]

Lawyers in legislatures will also reflect the larger social environment of which the legislature is a microcosm. In periods that are conservative, lawyers in politics will usually be conservative, just as in liberal periods liberal lawyers will be ascendant. The critical issue, of course, is whether lawyers are likely to prove a distinctively conservative element in legislatures if they are compared with nonlawyers. Derge, in his study of the 1957 Missouri House, did not find any significant differences between lawyers and nonlawyers on conservative and liberal positions in voting. He concludes from his data that "lawyers will be found on both liberal and conservative sides of political, social, and economic issues, and that the considerable influence of the lawyer group in the legislature will not be concentrated in support of, or opposition to, progressive legislation."[30]

In our own study of four legislatures in 1957—those of New Jersey, Ohio, Tennessee, and California—it was possible to measure the ideological stance of lawyers and nonlawyers in general by way of a short attitude scale.[31] Table 1.1 presents the results.

Table 1.1
Ideological Stance of Lawyers and Nonlawyers

	New Jersey		Ohio		Tennessee		California	
IDEOLOGY	L	NL	L	NL	L	NL	L	NL
Liberal	37%	32%	31%	24%	36%	20%	59%	40%
Moderate	29	32	25	24	30	35	19	34
Conservative	34	36	44	52	34	45	22	26
Total	100%	100%	100%	100%	100%	100%	100%	100%
Number	41	38	59	102	39	79	32	77

[29] Hurst, *op. cit.*, pp. 374–375.

[30] Derge, "The Lawyer as Decision-Maker," *op. cit.*, p. 431.

[31] For a description of the scale, see Appendix, pp. 152–153.

In all four state legislatures, greater proportions of the lawyers than of the nonlawyers actually scored "liberal," and greater proportions of the nonlawyers than of the lawyers scored "conservative." The differences between the two groups are, of course, not very great, though the patterns are consistent from one state to the next. For all practical purposes, then, lawyers and nonlawyers do not differ in their ideological stance; and, certainly, in these four legislatures in 1957 at least, lawyers were not more conservative than nonlawyers.

APPREHENSION NUMBER FOUR: THE TRAINING GAP

Lawyers may be better fitted by training and practice than other men to get themselves elected to public offices, but this fitness may not necessarily equip them to solve the complex social, economic, military, technical, and international problems that call for decisions. In particular, the criticism has been made that, given the lawyer's prominence in policy-making positions, the traditional law-school curriculum is deficient in two major respects. First, it ignores skills in negotiation, personnel management, and public relations, as well as in those ways of observation and thinking that are necessary to effective policy-making; and, second, it fails to educate the young lawyer in the clarification and selection of alternate values and goals as a necessary requisite for achieving a democratic commonwealth. The apprehension that lawyers may not be up to the demands made on them as policy-makers was forcefully voiced twenty years ago by Professors Harold D. Lasswell and Myres S. McDougal of the Yale University Law School. Their criticisms and suggestions for "professional training in the public interest" are much too extensive to be detailed here, but a one-paragraph answer to the question "what, then, are the essentials of adequate training for policy?" seems to summarize the burden of their argument:

> Effective policy-making (planning and implementation) depends on clear conception of goal, accurate calculation of probabilities, and adept application of knowledge of ways and means. We submit

that adequate training must therefore include experiences that aid the developing lawyer to acquire certain skills of thought: goal-thinking, trend-thinking, and scientific-thinking. The student needs to clarify his moral values (preferred events, social goals); he needs to orient himself in past trends and future probabilities; finally, he needs to acquire the scientific knowledge and skills necessary to implement objectives within the context of contemporary trends.[32]

Lasswell has suggested elsewhere that "often the nearest approach to a goal value to be sought by the lawyer is 'order.' " Yet, continues Lasswell, the lawyer "has an impact on the entire pattern of values and institutions. But he is not trained to think about these impacts or to relate them to a coherent and implicit set of assumptions about goal values, trends and conditions."[33] David Gold has pointed out that the lawyer's professional role as advocate—in which he finds himself sometimes on one, sometimes on the other side of the same fence—tends to free him from ideological commitment but also makes him more flexible in choosing goals:

. . . carried over into politics this approach would tend to make the lawyer more willing to operate in terms of any set of policy formulations. He becomes in general less goal-oriented and more means-oriented than the nonlawyer.[34]

Whether this is so we cannot say. But if Gold's speculation is accurate, it would seem to make concern over the training gap all the more pertinent. Of all the apprehensions voiced about the lawyer's role in public life, his possible "trained incapacity" to make decisions

---

[32] Harold D. Lasswell and Myres S. McDougal, "Legal Education and Public Policy: Professional Training in the Public Interest," in Harold D. Lasswell, *The Analysis of Political Behavior* (New York: Oxford University Press, 1948), p. 30. This epochal article was first published in *The Yale Law Journal* for March 1943.

[33] Harold D. Lasswell, *Power and Personality* (New York: W. W. Norton, 1948), pp. 135–136. See also Karl Krastin, "The Lawyer in Society—A Value Analysis," *Western Reserve Law Review*, VIII (September 1957), 409–455.

[34] David Gold, "Lawyers in Politics," *The Pacific Sociological Review*, IV (Fall 1961), 84.

in the public interest would seem to be the one most immediately relevant.

If lawyers do not get the training or have the skills necessary for effective performance of political roles, the question still remains whether those who are in political office are not exceptions to the rule. One might suppose that those who actively seek public office are likely to differ in values, interests, and orientations toward politics from those who do not. There may be a process of pre-selection that sorts lawyers into those who, because they are public-spirited or feel adequate to the task of government, enter positions of public trust, and those who prefer and stay in private careers. Whether lawyer-politicians do in fact differ from their brethren in private practice alone or in business enterprise can be determined only through appropriate comparative study.

CONCLUSION

This chapter has reviewed a number of apprehensions that seem to be at the base of either empirical studies or speculative essays concerning the lawyer's role in politics or public life. Of these apprehensions, that of "over-representation" proves least persuasive; yet it was most pervasive in past discussions of lawyers in politics. In itself it is not really a "problem" unless one entertains further assumptions of a normative kind about the nature of representation. It comes within the range of empirical proof or disproof only if the numerical strength of lawyers is assumed to affect policy outcomes or the functioning of politics in identifiable ways. One of these outcomes would be misuse of numerical predominance in the shaping of legislation in the interest of the legal profession rather than in the public interest. But this result is predicated on solidarity and cohesion among lawyers, a condition that seems not to be met. Another outcome would be an accentuation of whatever conservative tendencies might exist in a political institution, for lawyers as individuals are said to be conservative. But what evidence there is does not seem to indicate that, today at least, lawyers are any more conservative than nonlawyer politicians.

Yet, as one reviews the studies that have been made of the lawyer-politician, one is impressed by the pervasiveness of the assumptions made about over-representation and its attendant "evils"—even among those who do not find the lawyer-politician the political superman he is sometimes made out to be. But few studies transcend the implicit assumption that, somehow, lawyer-politicians will differ significantly from other politicians and that the difference is likely to affect policy outcomes in ways favorable to the interests of lawyers. Robert E. Agger, in an exceptionally perceptive essay, has stated this implicit assumption succinctly:

> The phenomenon of conservatism among lawyers, to the extent it exists, is not disturbing *per se*, but when political mechanisms for orderly social change are monopolized by lawyers and become mechanisms for personal power and reward—*whether harnessed to social change or to status quo*—the great number and influence of lawyers in politics deserves to be questioned.[35]

If apprehensions about the prominence of the legal profession in politics and the possible consequences of the lawyer's numerical predominance are not viable research approaches, does this mean that inquiry into the political careers of lawyers, their institutional position, and their political behavior is expendable? We think not. Rather, what seems to be expendable is not inquiry but only the ways in which the "problem" has been posed—by inference from highly generalized and largely unsubstantiated observations about the legal profession *in general*, and with the help of some fallacious assumptions about representation and consequent conditions. Such statements of the problem are not likely to yield very satisfactory knowledge about the lawyer's role in politics.

---

[35] Robert E. Agger, "Lawyers in Politics: The Starting Point for a New Research Program," *Temple Law Quarterly*, XXIX (Summer 1956), 439. Italics have been added.

Chapter 2

THE INSTITUTIONAL LINK

Of attempts to explain the affinity of law and politics as vocations, the oldest seeks to do so in institutional terms. Alexis de Tocqueville was the first who stated this type of analysis, in his classic treatise on America. He equates political rulership with the presumably high class position of the legal profession.[1] Related, but more subtle and sophisticated, is the explanation, best formulated by the German sociologist Max Weber, that attributes the predominance of the lawyer in political life to his evidently independent position in the modern capitalist economy.[2] A third institutional explanation, very simple but highly plausible, has been most fully articulated by the American political scientist Joseph A. Schlesinger. He has suggested that lawyers' almost complete monopoly of law enforcement offices, which is related to the administration of justice by the courts, places lawyers in a favorable position to occupy other political offices as well.[3] This chapter will deal with each of these institutional explanations and will appraise them in terms of immediately pertinent or inferentially relevant empirical data.

---

[1] Alexis de Tocqueville, *Democracy in America* (New York and London: Oxford University Press, 1947), pp. 171–177. This work was first published in France in two parts, in 1835 and 1840.

[2] Max Weber, "Politics as a Vocation," in H. H. Gerth and C. Wright Mills (eds.), *From Max Weber: Essays in Sociology* (New York: Oxford University Press, 1946), pp. 77–128. Weber's essay was first published in 1919.

[3] Joseph A. Schlesinger, "Lawyers and American Politics: A Clarified View," *Midwest Journal of Political Science*, I (May 1957), 26–39.

THE LAWYER IN THE SOCIAL STRUCTURE

It is always risky to extract from what is a closely reasoned argument, but the following excerpt from De Tocqueville's famous discussion seems to reflect accurately the gist of his point of view. De Tocqueville wrote:

> The government of democracy is favorable to the political power of lawyers; for when the wealthy, the noble, and the prince are excluded from the government, they are sure to occupy the highest stations, in their own right, as it were, since they are the only men of information and sagacity, beyond the sphere of the people, who can be the objects of popular choice.[4]

It is perhaps irrelevant to point out that De Tocqueville somewhat misjudged the lawyer's position in American public life, at least in the decades that followed the publication of his treatise. But, for the record, the historical situation will be briefly reviewed. At the time of the Revolution, and immediately thereafter, it is true—and attested to by their omnipresence in the making of the new nation—that lawyers had a relatively high status that accompanied the development of a strong legal profession in the wake of commercial and economic growth during the later eighteenth century.[5] But the lawyer's status declined in the years between 1830 and 1870, as a result of the de-professionalization of the bar. Hostility to all things English was partly responsible for this change. De Tocqueville's notion of a legal aristocracy was contrary to the basic beliefs and practices of Jacksonian democracy. The frontier age had no use for specialists in either private or public life. Law practice was considered a "natural right."[6] Educational requirements were drastically

---

[4] De Tocqueville, op. cit., pp. 172–173.

[5] Roscoe Pound, "The Legal Profession in America," Notre Dame Lawyer, XIX (June 1944), 334–353.

[6] W. Raymond Blackard, "The Demoralization of the Legal Profession in 19th Century America," Tennessee Law Review, XVI (April 1940), 314–323.

reduced, and "reading law" was, until after 1870 and the revival of professionalization, the proper mode of legal preparation.[7]

Even though De Tocqueville seems to have misjudged the temper of the new American democracy as it affected the role of the lawyer in the polity, his argument is eminently functional. He implied that there *must* be a class of persons in a democracy to run the government. The legal profession is well qualified to fulfill this function in the United States because there is no traditional American ruling class. Without denying that other characteristics peculiar to the legal profession also make politics attractive to lawyers, De Tocqueville presents a theoretically plausible explanation of the lawyer's prominence in politics: The legal profession fills institutionally and functionally necessary governing roles that cannot be left unoccupied. In a democracy the legal profession has no competition as an enlightened class because of the absence of an aristocracy and the unacceptability of the wealthy in governing roles. He summed up his argument:

> In America there are no nobles or men of letters, and the people is apt to mistrust the wealthy; lawyers consequently form the highest political class, and the most cultivated circle of society.[8]

The class interpretation of the lawyer's ascendancy in American political life has been restated recently, in modern terms and with considerably more caution, by Donald R. Matthews. He argues as follows: "Regardless of democratic institutions and values, political decision-makers will tend to be chosen from among those ranking high in America's system of social stratification."[9] He continues:

---

[7] Roscoe Pound, *The Lawyer from Antiquity to Modern Times* (St. Paul, Minn.: West Publishing Company, 1953), p. 236.

[8] De Tocqueville, *op. cit.*, p. 175. He continues, pointing out that because of their dominant position lawyers have "nothing to gain by innovation, which adds a conservative interest to their natural taste for public order." But this is another matter.

[9] Donald R. Matthews, *The Social Background of Political Decision-Makers* (Garden City, N.Y.: Doubleday & Company, 1954), p. 23.

"Lawyers meet what seems to be the first prerequisite of top-level political leadership: they are in a high-prestige occupation."[10] Of course, unlike De Tocqueville, Matthews is not committed to finding something that is not there. If the class hypothesis is relevant, Matthews asks, how does it happen that persons in other high-status occupations—physicians, businessmen, or scientists—do not fill political positions in any proportion comparable to that of lawyers? His answer is, first, that certain skills prevalent among lawyers fit them especially well to careers in politics; second, there is "the position of the legal profession in American society that must be considered as another factor contributing to the lawyer's political dominance." Matthews continues:

> Unlike many other countries the United States has never had a landed aristocracy with a tradition of public service. While most political decision-makers enjoy high-prestige positions, few are the possessors of inherited wealth. In a highly competitive society in which occupational success is the most highly valued goal for the ambitious, who can with the least danger leave their jobs for the tremendous risks of a political career? Among the high-prestige occupations the answer seems to be the lawyer.[11]

The quotation shows that Matthews' argument subtly shifts from the lawyer's class position as an explanation to his role in the economy. This is understandable; for Matthews, class or status is only one factor contributing to the lawyer's predominance in politics. As he points out, "more than high social status is necessary in order to have high political opportunities."[12]

What is the viability of the class or social status argument, whether in De Tocqueville's projective outlook or in Matthews' circumspect view? Such concepts as class, social status, and prestige are

---

[10] *Ibid.*, p. 30.

[11] *Ibid.*, p. 31.

[12] *Ibid.*, pp. 31–32. Matthews continues, summing his explanation: "Some positions of high social status may actually be a detriment to the politically ambitious. But where high prestige is combined with training in interpersonal relations, easy access to politics, and 'dispensability,' as is the case for the lawyers, the result is a dominant position in American politics."

highly ambiguous and unstable in usage, and one should not employ them unless one indicates just what empirical referents they point to and what operations are to be performed in assembling relevant data. Nevertheless, before looking at some data, the class character of the legal profession should be discussed briefly.

That lawyers in America do not constitute a class in De Tocqueville's sense hardly requires demonstration, but what of their social status or prestige? In a social system as heterogeneous as is that of the United States, an appraisal of the social prestige of an occupation is extremely difficult to come by. Some bits of information are pertinent to such appraisal. In a survey of occupational prestige ratings conducted by the National Opinion Research Center in 1947, lawyers were tied in the rankings in fifteenth place, along with architects, chemists, dentists, members of boards of directors of large corporations, nuclear physicists, and priests.[13] These rankings were based on quite different degrees of knowledge of an occupation's "general standing" in the community or society. Although the average proportion of respondents unable to rate an occupation was four per cent, there was a great variation in the range of their lack of knowledge. For instance, though lawyers and nuclear physicists both ended up in fifteenth place, respondents unable to rate the lawyer numbered fewer than one per cent, whereas those unable to rate the nuclear physicist totaled 51 per cent.[14] Ratings might vary a good deal with respondents' demographic characteristics. For instance, Southern respondents gave lower ratings to the lawyer than did residents of the Northeast.[15]

It would seem that, if ranking of occupations is technically so difficult, unstable, and ambiguous, it is hardly possible to make any kind of reliable summary statement about an occupation's prestige as an index of its social status. Clarity concerning the class character of a profession would seem prerequisite to a class analysis of its

---

[13] Albert J. Reiss, Jr., *Occupations and Social Status* (New York: The Free Press of Glencoe, 1961), p. 54.

[14] *Ibid.*, p. 12.

[15] *Ibid.*, p. 168.

political perspective and behavior. But the legal profession's status is not only ambiguous externally; it is also ambiguous internally. Quite different evaluations are given to particular types of lawyers by outsiders as well as by members of the profession itself. As mentioned earlier, lawyers range from the often highly specialized "corporation lawyer" (possibly in firms some of which hire associates only from families listed in the *Social Register*) to lawyers in small partnerships and the great bulk of lawyers who still practice alone.[16] To these should be added lawyers directly employed by business firms, labor unions, government, and law schools. Moreover, the particular lawyer's status is often determined less by his occupation than by his ethnic background or group affiliation, notably in the case of Negroes and Jews.[17]

When such indicators of social class as income or education are taken into account, it is difficult to say what an "average lawyer" is. The more than 250,000 lawyers in the United States vary among themselves a great deal in both education and income. In 1954, the median income of lawyers was $7,800; a third of the lawyers in private practice, however, made less than $5,000 a year, while a fifth of them made more than $15,000.[18] As the American sociologist Bernard Barber has observed, "when the earnings of lawyers range from a few thousand dollars a year to a few hundreds of thousands, then it is likely that their social class positions vary greatly and it will not do to lump them all together under the single position of 'lawyer.' "[19] Moreover, as late as 1951 only about 49 per cent of all lawyers for whom data were available had received college degrees

---

[16] Albert P. Blaustein and Charles O. Porter, *The American Lawyer: A Summary of the Survey of the Legal Profession* (Chicago: University of Chicago Press, 1954), p. 8.

[17] C. Ray Jeffery, "The Legal Profession," in F. James Davis, Henry H. Foster, C. Ray Jeffery, and E. Eugene Davis, *Society and the Law: New Meanings for an Old Profession* (New York: The Free Press of Glencoe, 1962), pp. 317–331.

[18] Maurice Liebenberg, "Income of Lawyers in the Postwar Period," *Survey of Current Business*, XXXVI (December 1956), 26–36.

[19] Bernard Barber, *Social Stratification: A Comparative Analysis of Structure and Process* (New York: Harcourt, Brace and Company, 1957), p. 109.

(though about 82 per cent had attended college).[20] It is likely that the percentage of college graduates has since increased, but lawyers still differ a great deal in the quality of their educational backgrounds.

Even though the legal profession cannot be considered as a class, as De Tocqueville thought it could, or even spoken of in class terms without doing injustice to its social heterogeneity, data from the four states of this study show that lawyer-politicians are evidently recruited from the upper income and educational strata of their profession and, as a group, are better off financially and better educated than nonlawyer-politicians. Even so rough a classification as that used in Table 2.1 shows considerable differences in income between lawyer-legislators and nonlawyer-legislators from state to state.

Table 2.1
Income of Lawyers and Nonlawyers in 1957

	New Jersey		Ohio		Tennessee		California	
INCOME	L	NL	L	NL	L	NL	L	NL
Under $5,000	0%	0%	0%	0%	10%	23%	0%	0%
$5,000–10,000	5	21	21	53	44	44	3	24
$10,000–20,000	44	55	51	33	28	27	58	44
Over $20,000	49	19	25	11	18	6	30	28
Not ascertained	2	5	3	3	0	0	9	4
Total	100%	100%	100%	100%	100%	100%	100%	100%
Number	41	38	59	103	39	81	33	80

The figures presented in the table include legislators' annual legislative salary, and allowance must be made for this accordingly.[21] In California, annual base pay was $6,000; in New Jersey and Ohio,

---

[20] Blaustein and Porter, *op. cit.*, pp. 192–193, Table 14.

[21] The interview question from which the income figures come reads as follows: "Now, including your legislative salary, into which of these four income groups would you say your total annual income falls?" (Less than $5,000; $5,000–10,000; $10,000–20,000; over $20,000) The reasons for asking the question in this fashion were: (a) by asking respondents to place themselves in a rough category, it was hoped that they would be more willing to cooperate

$5,000; and in Tennessee, only $375.[22] It is quite clear, then, that the differences in total income that can be noted between California, New Jersey, and Ohio on the one hand, and Tennessee on the other hand, are in part accentuated by the much higher legislative salaries in the three "northern" states. Although–if income is taken as an indicator–all lawyer-legislators are "middle class," vague as this term may be, the distributions in the four states suggest that lawyers may belong to quite different income strata. Some implications of these income figures for the political behavior of lawyer-politicians will be discussed in the next section.

Further, lawyers who serve in state legislatures seem to be better educated than nonlawyer-politicians. In all four states the number of lawyers who had never been at college, whether they graduated or not, was quite small, and lawyers differed considerably in this respect from the nonlawyers. Great proportions of the lawyers had been to college, and some had received, in addition to their legal training, other advanced education. If education were to be used as an index of social class, we should find clear indication in Table 2.2 that lawyer-legislators are better educated than their nonlawyer legislative colleagues.

We conclude from our discussion of the lawyer's prestige ranking in American society generally, and from the income and educational data just presented, that, even if the legal profession were a socially

---

than if they had been directly asked to give the exact amount of their income; (b) respondents were asked to include their legislative salary in total income to make it even easier for them to give an answer on a topic where invasion of privacy might have been resented by some–as, indeed, it was.

[22] In appraising legislative salary, allowance must be made for differences in time demands and other factors, such as travel from and to the state capital. As inspection of Table 3.4 of *The Legislative System*, p. 51, will show, Tennessee legislators are clearly "underprivileged," while New Jersey legislators are exceptionally favored, compared even with those in California and Ohio. They meet on only one day a week and have very short distances to travel. Californians, on the other hand, have longer distances to journey, and some must even move their families to the capital. By way of compensation, California legislators receive a per diem allowance and an interim travel grant, as well as private secretarial support. Ohio legislators receive a mileage allowance that is generous, though most of it goes into paying hotel bills.

Table 2.2

Education of Lawyers and Nonlawyers

	New Jersey		Ohio		Tennessee		California	
EDUCATION	L	NL	L	NL	L	NL	L	NL
No college (but law school)*	10%	26%	0%	36%	10%	38%	3%	24%
College (complete and incomplete)	68	53	95	44	80	38	94	53
Law school and other graduate school	22	8	5	14	10	12	3	20
Other	0	13	0	6	0	12	0	3
Total	100%	100%	100%	100%	100%	100%	100%	100%
Number	41	38	59	103	39	81	33	80

* These are respondents who had not attended an undergraduate college but who had received law training in institutions not requiring an A.B. degree as a prerequisite of law training.

homogeneous occupational group, which it is not, the lawyer's class position is highly heterogeneous. It seems highly questionable, therefore, to attribute the dominance of the lawyer in politics to the alleged high-status position of his profession in the American society. On the other hand, it would seem that high educational attainment may well give the lawyer an advantage in gaining access to political office—not because he may have gone to law school, however, but because he seems generally better educated than his nonlawyer colleagues.

THE LAWYER IN THE ECONOMIC STRUCTURE

As noted earlier, the flowering of the legal profession in the United States tended to coincide with the rise of commerce and industry. This occurred at least twice—in the wake of economic development in the second part of the eighteenth century, and again a hundred years later. The particular roles that the lawyer was called upon to take as a lawyer under conditions of economic growth will be discussed in Chapter 4. The present observations deal with the particular characteristics of economic organization in the private-property order that seem to make a political career especially attractive to members of the legal profession.

The classic argument—an exceptionally tight one that is difficult to summarize—was expounded by Max Weber. His starting point is the distinction between two types of politician—one who lives "off" politics, and one who lives "for" politics. In the absence of a regular income, the politician may make his living as a party official or as a functionary in government, or even by taking fees and bribes. On the other hand, an independent and steady source of income may allow him to live "for" politics. The distinction, in Weber's formulation, is not an invidious one:

> The rule is, rather, that man does both, at least in thought, and certainly does both in practice. He who lives "for" politics makes politics his life, in an internal sense. Either he enjoys the naked possession of power he exerts, or he nourishes his inner balance and self-feeling by the consciousness that his life has *meaning* in the service of a "cause." In this internal sense, every sincere man who lives for a cause also lives off this cause.[23]

In other words, living "off" politics does not necessarily preclude the politician from devoted public service, just as living "for" politics does not inevitably prohibit him from exploiting his position in order to make a living. Weber emphasizes that the distinction is basically economic:

> Under the dominance of the private property order, some—if you wish—very trivial preconditions must exist in order for a person to be able to live "for" politics in this economic sense. Under normal conditions, the politician must be economically independent of the in-

---

[23] Weber, *op. cit.*, p. 84.

come politics can bring him. This means, quite simply, that the politician must be wealthy or must have a personal position in life which yields a sufficient income.[24]

But an independent income is not the only condition of living "for" politics:

> The professional politician must also be economically "dispensable," that is, his income must not depend upon the fact that he constantly and personally places his ability and thinking entirely, or at least by far predominantly, in the service of economic acquisition.[25]

Neither the worker nor the entrepreneur, Weber continues, is economically dispensable in this sense; each is as little dispensable as the medical doctor. At this point Weber introduces his argument for the peculiar availability of the lawyer in politics. "For purely organizational reasons"—that is, reasons of organization in the private property order,

> it is easier for the lawyer to be dispensable; and therefore the lawyer has played an incomparably greater, and often even a dominant, role as a professional politician.[26]

Weber does not rest his explanation of the lawyer's dominance in politics on the economic argument alone. But, as Reinhard Bendix has pointed out, "for Weber, lawyers are the prototype of the modern professional politician. They are available for political activities in economic terms. Through arrangements with their associates they can free their time for politics and continue to receive an income or at least can expect to return to a secure and profitable profession when their political activity has come to an end."[27]

Weber's analysis dates from more than forty years ago and was made in the context of European politics. Does it hold in the United

---

[24] *Ibid.*, pp. 84–85.

[25] *Ibid.*, p. 85.

[26] *Ibid.*

[27] Reinhard Bendix, *Max Weber: An Intellectual Portrait* (Garden City, N.Y.: Doubleday & Company, 1960), p. 436.

States, where few politicians are possessors of inherited wealth? To answer this question, it is important to keep apart the two aspects of Weber's argument—"economic independence" and "economic dispensability." This is not always done. In the United States, wrote V. O. Key, Jr.,

> . . . the high incidence of lawyers among the politically influential provides a base of economic independence; the defeated politician can always find a few clients. Extensive reliance on part-time, amateur politicians in representative bodies and in many governing commissions has assured an economic cushion for many political activists. The custom of making many such offices economically unattractive has, in effect, required that they be filled by persons with an economic base independent of the public treasury.[28]

But could it not be that lawyers might seek political office to supplement their private income precisely where political office calls for only part-time involvement and where public salaries for such part-time work are relatively high, as in California, New Jersey, or Ohio? We noted in the previous section that lawyer-legislators, though reasonably well off, come from widely varying income strata. Later chapters will show that at least some lawyer-legislators may seek office not because they are well-to-do, but because their legislative salary supplements their private income and, in fact, constitutes a substantial part of their total income. And some lawyer-legislators may give up their political career because they cannot afford it.

On the other hand, the "dispensability" argument may yet be appropriate. As Matthews put it:

> The law changes relatively slowly, and a politician is in a position to keep up with many of the changes in the law while active in politics. The lawyer, either in individual practice or in a law firm of a few members, is dispensable. He can most easily combine his occupation, on a part-time basis, with political activity.[29]

---

[28] V. O. Key, Jr., *Public Opinion and American Democracy* (New York: Alfred A. Knopf, 1961), p. 540.

[29] Donald R. Matthews, *U.S. Senators and Their World* (Chapel Hill: University of North Carolina Press, 1960), pp. 34–35.

Before introducing some of our data, it is important to emphasize that the overwhelming majority of state legislators in this study do not consider themselves "professional" politicians in either of Weber's two senses of the term. Only 20 of the 474 respondents in the four states (about four per cent) gave "politician" or "legislator" as their occupation. As stated elsewhere,

> . . . for most of them political work was a part-time career super-imposed on their ordinary callings. But neither were many what Weber called "occasional politicians" for whom politics is only an avocation. . . . Rather, American state legislators would seem in most cases to be mixed-type politicians who are neither devoted pro-fessionals nor inspired amateurs. But if they do not live off politics or for politics, they are, nevertheless, very much *in* politics as something more than an occasional incident in an otherwise non-political career.[30]

Needless to say, perhaps, it is unlikely that in an interview of the kind that was conducted respondents would acknowledge candidly that they sought office because of the financial advantage their legis-lative salary might give them. Few would say, as one respondent said, "The big stimulus was economic; I got my first political job after one year as a practicing lawyer." And few would say, as an-other admitted in an afterthought to another response, that political work is "also good during lean years of practice." More often the directly economic motive would be concealed, as for instance in this response: "My father told me that it would be good for law practice, long ago." On the other hand, the paucity of such comments does not permit the conclusion that the legislative salary is *not* an attraction to office-seekers. Just how many lawyer-legislators would have ad-mitted to this, however, if they had been asked a direct, closed question, we cannot say.

Among the most familiar and plausible "economic" explanations that have been offered for the lawyer's interest in public office is that political activity "can be a positive advantage to his occupational advancement—free and professionally legitimate advertising, con-

---

[30] Wahlke *et al.*, *The Legislative System*, p. 76.

tacts, and opportunity to meet important lawyers of his region result from his political activities."[31] Some of the respondents in the
present study confirmed this explanation:

> Well, real frankly, I graduated from law school in the fall. I
> couldn't take the bar exam 'til spring. I had no practice to go to.
> Running for political office seemed expedient. Once again, selfishly
> speaking, an attorney is prohibited from advertising. I thought it was
> better to go around meeting people through politics.

> It was not so much for the political aspect of it. I went into politics
> really for selfish reasons. I'd been practicing law for less than a year,
> and this is a very good way to become better known in the com-
> munity. Consequently, that was my initial reason for going into
> politics.

> That's difficult to answer. I was out of law school and thought of
> it as a measure of advertising myself before the public. That was the
> prime motive.

A few respondents in all states pointed out that a legal career and
a political career could easily go hand in hand, as follows:

> Because of its close relation to law practice, I could continue prac-
> ticing law. It serves my interests the best. With another full-time
> elective position I'd have to give up my practice. This way I can still
> do everything.

A few lawyer-legislators were "sent" to the legislature as "agents" of
their law firms:

> While in law partnership, it was decided that I would be the first
> one in the firm to run for office. . . . I was then chosen by the senior
> partners in the firm as having the best chance.

If lawyers enter politics in order to advertise their name and
practice, it would seem reasonable to expect them to do so at a
relatively young age—in fact, soon after they have left law school
and before they have "established" themselves. The median age of all

---

[31] Matthews, *U.S. Senators*, p. 35.

legislators serving in the four states in 1957 was about fifty.[32] If legislators are grouped with the age of fifty as a dividing line, an overwhelming 85 per cent of the lawyers, but only 40 per cent of the nonlawyers, fall in the younger category. Table 2.3 presents the median age of lawyer- and nonlawyer-legislators in the four states. In all states lawyer-legislators as a group are clearly younger than non-

Table 2.3
Median Age of Lawyer- and Nonlawyer-Legislators

	New Jersey		Ohio		Tennessee		California	
	L	NL	L	NL	L	NL	L	NL
Median age	46.0	49.3	39.4	56.0	30.3	48.2	43.2	54.0

lawyer-legislators. On the other hand, very few of the lawyers in these legislatures are also under thirty (10 out of 474)—that is, of an age at which, presumably, the need for free professional publicity is greatest. This fact might explain why so few of the lawyer-legislators spontaneously mentioned the matter of publicity. Indeed, if one acknowledges that running for office costs money, young lawyers, unless they are subsidized by party or friends, cannot afford to run before they have established themselves, much as they might wish to in order to make themselves known in their communities. In general, it would seem that while holding public office is possibly advantageous to some lawyers, it is not a compelling road either to riches or to public notice. Plausible as the explanation is that lawyers are so visible in politics because they may directly gain from seeking and holding public office, much more proof is needed before this explanation can be accepted.

If it be true that the young lawyer goes into politics in order to advertise his practice, then he would seem to be free to retire and return to his private practice once he has advertised it. Yet, it cannot be simply assumed that lawyers will serve for shorter periods

---

[32] See Wahlke *et al., op. cit.*, p. 491, Table A-13: Age of Legislators in 1957.

than nonlawyers. Tenure and turnover in state legislatures are affected by many factors other than occupation or the concomitants of occupation; of prime importance among these factors is defeat at the polls, in primaries and general elections.[33] And the data are rather inconclusive. As Table 2.4 shows,.in two states—New Jersey and Tennessee—practically no difference exists in length of service between lawyer- and nonlawyer-legislators; in Ohio the lawyers served only a little less long than the nonlawyers. Only in California is there a large difference. Some of the legislators' own "subjective"

Table 2.4
Median Length of Service of Lawyers and Nonlawyers

	New Jersey		Ohio		Tennessee		California	
	L	NL	L	NL	L	NL	L	NL
Median years of service	3.9	3.8	4.3	5.1	2.2	2.3	2.8	6.8

reasons for withdrawal from public service—some of which are "economic"—will follow presently. In any case, the data on length of service do not support the notion that lawyers are any more "economically integrated" into the structure of politics than are nonlawyers because the financial advantages of political service are easier to come by for them than for nonlawyers.

One can still argue reasonably that, even though the "publicity hypothesis" may not generally hold, lawyers will hang onto their positions, if they can, in order to continue to promote their private practice. From time to time legislators must, at intervals specified by law, decide whether or not they want to stay in office, cease running for office, or seek another office. Table 2.5 presents the respondents' best guesses about whether or not they will seek reelection to the state legislature.

---

[33] See various studies of Charles S. Hyneman, including "Tenure and Turnover in the Indiana General Assembly," *American Political Science Review*, XXXII (February and April 1938), 51–67, 311–331.

Table 2.5
Expectation to Run Again for Legislature

	New Jersey		Ohio		Tennessee		California	
EXPECTATION	L	NL	L	NL	L	NL	L	NL
Run again	78%	73%	53%	65%	30%	36%	79%	61%
Perhaps	12	11	27	17	39	37	9	15
Not run again	10	13	12	10	28	22	6	9
Not ascertained	0	3	8	8	3	5	6	15
Total	100%	100%	100%	100%	100%	100%	100%	100%
Number	41	38	59	103	39	81	33	80

Though state legislature turnover is high, the table shows that in the three states where annual salary is $5,000 or better the majority of legislators plans to run again. In Tennessee, of course, where legislative salary is quite low, continued legislative service is not highly valued. But no pattern characterizes the responses of lawyers and nonlawyers from state to state. Lawyers do not seem more or less committed than nonlawyers to a continued legislative career. The fact that some respondents equivocated or gave "no" responses does not mean, of course, that all of them were planning to leave politics. Some who gave these answers were anticipating another, possibly a "higher," political office.

It is interesting to note that, of those who were planning to run again, only a few gave "economic reasons" for doing so. Quotations from the interviews with lawyers illustrate this response:

Because of my experience, I think I can help. My position in life allows me to devote time to it. I'm financially stable. I like meeting people. I like to be in—each bill is a crossword puzzle and has something wrong with it. I like to find out what's wrong with it. It's an interesting job, *financially good.*

I'm interested in it; I enjoy it. I commute from 46 miles north of here, so there's opportunity to carry on my practice in the morning at home. It doesn't interfere and probably *helps my private business*, if anything.

I need the money. No, take that out. I have continued interest. I do have an interest in industrial relations and education. I'm interested in all that junk that goes on. Any attorney would be interested.

Moreover, in looking at the reasons given for not running again for the legislative seat presently held, two arguments immediately relevant to this economic discussion stand out: Some respondents mentioned directly economic reasons for not wanting to run again; some felt that they had served long enough. Since the second point was often made in connection with the first, it is reasonable to suppose that, even if it is mentioned alone, it is only another way of saying that legislative service is not economically worth while. The following comments from the protocols are suggestive:

I think it's time I devoted myself to my law practice. Being in the legislature has *hurt my practice* and *cost me money*. Also, I don't think anyone should make a career of serving in the legislature. You do your part and then make room for the next guy.

I don't think I should stay too long. The law is my career. . . . A political career is too uncertain and hazardous. *Law practice is more secure.*

Probably I'll continue to run for a while. I wouldn't be sorry, though, if I were asked to leave voluntarily. There are a number of other pressures such as the time I have to spend away from my family and *away from my business.* I've no burning desire to stick with this.

There are no startling differences in this respect between the few lawyers and nonlawyers who did not plan to run again. Insofar as there is a difference, lawyers seem to be inclined to emphasize the economic loss rather than the economic gain involved in their legislative service.

What about the lawyer's "dispensability," then? Is not the fact that more lawyers than participants in other occupations are members of legislative bodies *prima facie* evidence of their dispensability? Two types of response are relevant. First, in connection with giving reasons for not seeking their *present* legislative job again, a few respondents, both lawyers and nonlawyers, mentioned the "demands of their job" as preventing them from running again. Second, in giving reasons for not seeking *another* office, both gave the same type of "job demands." But the data are insufficiently complete to permit any categorical statement about whether lawyers are, for occupational reasons, any more dispensable than are nonlawyers. Again, some quotations will illustrate lawyers' feelings in the matter:

> I feel like I would like to run someday for something higher, such as Congress, but I have to weigh what it will do to my law practice. I have a problem, I'm not in a good law association. I might lose a lot of professional fees. I may have to get out on my own. It would be wonderful to go into politics if I had a good partner, but I hate to give up my law practice. I'll try to work things out.

> You take so much time for legislation you have none for your own business. A legislator is neither fish nor fowl, neither lawyer nor full-time official. I'd do better at home and there's a future there.

Comparison of lawyers and nonlawyers in the four state legislatures does not provide very convincing evidence for the lawyer's alleged economic independence or occupational dispensability as major institutional reasons for his ubiquity in politics. On the contrary, it would seem that lawyers are as willing and ready as nonlawyers to live "off" politics if doing so does not interfere with their law practice. There is no reason to suppose that lawyers differ in significant ways from nonlawyers in their ability to return to private business once they leave politics, whether they do so voluntarily or whether they are defeated at the polls. It is well to keep in mind, however, that the nonlawyers, too, represent occupations that might be considered "dispensable"—some are real estate men, insurance people, tire dealers, public relations specialists, and so on. Rather than asking whether there is something in the economic circumstances that makes the members of these occupations, like those of the legal profession, go into politics, one might perhaps ask what it is that makes members of other occupations *not* seek public office. It is doubtful that such inquiry would discover their presumed economic *de*pendence or occupational *in*dispensability as major reasons.

THE LAWYER IN THE POLITICAL STRUCTURE

The modern state is a "legal state" governed by the "rule of law." As Weber pointed out in discussing "politics as a vocation," the trained jurist—the man educated in Roman jurisprudence—

> . . . has been of decisive significance for the Continent's whole political structure. The tremendous after-effect of Roman law, as transformed by the late Roman bureaucratic state, stands out in nothing more clearly than the fact that everywhere the resolution of political management in the direction of the evolving rational state has been borne by trained jurists. This also occurred in England. . . .[34]

Not only the absolute state but also the revolutionary state owes its engineering to the work of lawyers. In its occupational composition, Weber noted, the French Revolutionary Assembly of 1789 included—"although the members of the Assembly were elected through equal franchise—a single proletarian, very few bourgeois enterprisers, but jurists of all sorts, *en masse*. . . . Since the French Revolution, the modern lawyer and modern democracy absolutely belong together."[35] In revolutionary America, too, as mentioned earlier, lawyers played a prominent role in the founding of the United States, and they have played a dominant role in constitutional engineering ever since.

Historical description serves as a useful background to functional analysis. Of more interest in political interpretation is the fact, inci-

---

[34] Weber, *op. cit.*, p. 93.

[35] *Ibid.*, p. 94.

dentally noted by Harold D. Lasswell and his associates, that "possessing a practical monopoly in the West of one type of administration —the courts—the lawyers have another foothold on the political ladder."[36] This observation was recently revived by Joseph A. Schlesinger in a solid study of the political careers of American state governors between 1870 and 1950.

As Schlesinger rightly suggests, the notion that lawyers are predominant in politics because they have requisite political skills and qualities is really a form of residual explanation. Lawyers may or may not make better politicians than others, but "officeholding in itself proves only that lawyers are acceptable to the electorate." The lawyers' distinct advantage "in the public office structure of the United States is their monopoly of those offices involved in the administration of law through the courts."[37] What makes for the lawyer's ubiquity in politics is not simply his specific occupation but his hold on law enforcement offices, which give him a competitive advantage not enjoyed by his brethren who do not fill public offices. The easy interchange of personnel between the law enforcement hierarchy and all the other branches of government "leaves the occupational market for politicians in a state of imperfect competition, due to the lawyer's control over a major avenue to public office."[38] Schlesinger found that "of all the lawyer governors, approximately a third advanced directly from a law enforcement position. It would appear that for these lawyer governors the law enforcement position rather than their occupation was the significant factor in their advancement to the governorship."[39]

What is true of such executive politicians as state governors need not be true, of course, of legislative politicians. Yet, in the state legislative arena, too, the contrast between lawyers and nonlawyers

---

[36] Harold D. Lasswell, Daniel Lerner, and C. Easton Rothwell, *The Comparative Study of Elites* (Stanford: Stanford University Press, 1952), p. 18.

[37] Schlesinger, *op. cit.*, p. 31.

[38] *Ibid.*, p. 32.

[39] *Ibid.*

who had held a law enforcement office of one kind or another prior
to their legislative service is marked. As Table 2.6 shows, from 27 to

Table 2.6
Type of Previous Office Held by Lawyers and Nonlawyers*

TYPE OF OFFICE	New Jersey		Ohio		Tennessee		California	
	L	NL	L	NL	L	NL	L	NL
Judicial and law enforcement	32%	5%	27%	4%	31%	2%	36%	4%
Legislative	41	55	19	46	31	30	18	41
Executive	19	37	12	27	15	26	15	25
None	36	34	49	40	39	57	49	46
Number	41	38	59	103	39	81	33	80

* Percentages total more than 100 because respondents could have held more
than one such office before becoming state legislators.

36 per cent of the lawyers, but in no case more than 5 per cent of the
nonlawyers, had held judicial office before running for their legislative job. In this regard, then, as in the case of state governors, the
lawyers' monopoly of law enforcement offices seems to give them a
competitive advantage over nonlawyers in filling legislative positions.

On the other hand, this clearly does not mean that lawyers have
an absolute advantage over nonlawyers when it comes to becoming
state legislators. Table 2.6 shows that in all four states greater proportions of the nonlawyers than of the lawyers had held either other
legislative posts or executive positions before entering the legislature.
In other words, the advantage lawyers have that stems from their
monopoly of legal offices is clearly offset by the advantage nonlawyers have in holding legislative and executive offices. That this is
so appears from the numbers who had held no office before entering
the state legislature. In each of two states, New Jersey and California, the proportion of lawyers without any previous office experience is greater than the proportion of nonlawyers, but only

minimally so; in Ohio, it is somewhat greater. Only in Tennessee did considerably more of the nonlawyers have no other governmental experience at all, giving the lawyers a clear advantage. It seems that offices other than those connected with law enforcement may serve equally well either as springboards or as routes of a political career that, at least momentarily, leads to state legislative service.[40]

CONCLUSION

This chapter has reviewed a number of institutional interpretations of the lawyer's prominence in politics. Each of them is plausible, but none of them provides either necessary or sufficient bases for inferences about the attractiveness that politics seems to have for lawyers. All of them may be relevant in some cases, or perhaps even in many cases. The next chapter will examine the political career as a possible nexus between law as a profession and politics as a vocation, for in this connection comparison between lawyers and nonlawyers may suggest why molar institutional explanations do not yield very satisfactory results.

---

[40] This is also supported by Matthews' data on U.S. Senators. Though more of his sample of Senators (28 per cent) held judicial as first office achieved, 21 per cent, for instance, began their careers as state legislators; 14 per cent, as local elective officials; another 14 per cent, as administrators. See Matthews, *U.S. Senators*, p. 51, Table 22. And only 22 per cent of the lawyer-Senators had held a law enforcement office before entering the Senate, while others had held a variety of other political positions. See *ibid.*, p. 56, Table 28.

Chapter 3

THE CAREER NEXUS

*In a country so liberally blessed as is the United States with constitu-*tions and charters on at least three levels of government—federal, state, and local—the fetish of judicialism tends to obscure the fact that laws are, at bottom, instruments of politics. This did not escape that keen observer of the American Commonwealth, the Englishman James Bryce. Like De Tocqueville before him, Bryce was impressed by the visibility of lawyers in politics. The lawyers, he wrote, "are of all classes that which has most to do with politics. From their ranks comes a large part, probably a half, and the better educated half, of the professional politicians."[1] In trying to explain this, Bryce gave great weight not only to the attorney's need to watch current legisla-tion but also to the fact that the lawyer must be familiar with at least two constitutions—that of the federal government and that of his par-ticular state. For this reason, the study of law might lead to a height-ened interest in politics. Interest in one, Bryce implied, leads to interest in the other. Law and politics are compatible professions, and legal study leads to interest and activity in public affairs.

This is, of course, one of the conventional explanations for the affinity of law and politics as vocations. But at best it can be only a partial explanation. The lawyer's interest in politics may well stem from his legal study or from his legal aspirations in jurisdictions where appointment to judgeships is elective or politically controlled.

---

[1] James Bryce, *The American Commonwealth* (rev. ed.; New York: The Mac-millan Company, 1911), II, 306.

But most lawyers do not enter politics, and many are not interested in politics even from a professional point of view. Legal education, it would seem, is neither a necessary nor a sufficient cause of the affinity of law and politics as vocations (though this is not to deny that, for other reasons, the lawyer-politician may not have certain advantages over the nonlawyer in his pursuit of politics). But, although Bryce gave the conventional explanation, he was not a conventional observer. In another connection he implied—unfortunately, without much further elaboration—that the compatibility of law and politics as professions might derive from a primary orientation toward politics rather than from a study of law. "Law," he wrote, "is of course the business which best fits in with politics."[2] In other words, politics may well be an avocation for lawyers or may even become their main profession, stimulated by their study of law; but the reverse might also be the case—law may be a convenient occupation for budding young politicians.

Bryce's observation would seem to call for fairly detailed investigation of the political life history of lawyers who have made their way into politics. On the basis of some of the interview protocols, the notion of the lawyer-politician's primary interest in politics seems not at all implausible. At least some statements made by lawyer-legislators are suggestive. That these statements come from a single, open-ended question that did not direct the respondent's answers at all augments their value. The following statements are not offered as "proof" but merely as material illustrative of Bryce's suggestive observation:

> I was always interested in it. I picked law as my major in college *with an eye on politics.* I started out as a chemistry major, but switched to law after my first year.

> I'm from a political family. You might say that we've always been in it. *When I was still young* I used to campaign door-to-door. Well, originally I wanted to be a doctor, but I went into law instead.

---

[2] *Ibid.*, p. 65.

> I have always been interested in politics. I'd say this was true since
> I was about ten years old. I guess it was a natural interest. I remem-
> ber what was probably my first exposure, when I was ten: that was
> listening to the Republican national convention. Yes, that was the
> starting point. For me, *this interest seemed to be a natural thing.*

As the first two quotations indicate, these respondents actually
switched their occupational choices—in one case from chemistry, in
the other from medicine—in order, evidently, to enter a private
profession that would facilitate their entry into politics. For them, as
for the third respondent here cited, politics was a "natural thing."
Indeed, as a statement made by a nonlawyer shows, politics may be
a substitute for a legal career if, for one reason or another, the latter
is blocked as an avenue into politics:

> When I came out of high school, I wanted to be a lawyer. My
> parents are religious folks and wanted me to be a preacher. That's
> why I never went to college, got that job with the coal company. But
> I was always interested in politics. I kept close to it and watched it on
> the city level, was active in campaigns, but never was an organization
> worker.

These quotations and others to be cited later suggest that it may
be worthwhile to compare systematically the political careers of
lawyer- and nonlawyer-legislators. For the concept of "political
career" implies that success in politics, within the limits of condition-
ing circumstances, can be purposefully planned and achieved.

THE POLITICAL SOCIALIZATION OF LAWYERS

If lawyers in politics come first to politics and then to law as a convenient occupation that permits them to pursue their political in-
clinations, one should expect that more of the lawyers than of the
nonlawyers will recall early experiences in and with politics. Table
3.1 presents some relevant data. Two aspects of the table stand out:
In all four states, more of the lawyers than of the nonlawyers located
their earliest interest in politics in the childhood or grammar-school

Table 3.1
Time of Earliest Interest in Politics

TIME	New Jersey		Ohio		Tennessee		California	
	L	NL	L	NL	L	NL	L	NL
Childhood	29%	16%	44%	29%	44%	27%	53%	34%
Adolescence	10	11	14	16	18	7	25	13
College (or equivalent time)	17	3	12	14	8	6	6	9
Post-college (or equivalent time)	12	16	8	12	15	20	9	20
On entry into politics	10	21	15	28	5	17	6	23
Not ascertained	22	34	7	2	10	21	1	1
Total	100%	100%	100%	100%	100%	100%	100%	100%
Number	41	38	59	103	39	81	33	80

period of their lives; and fewer of the lawyers than of the non-lawyers consistently mentioned post-college years or equivalent periods and the circumstance of their active entry into politics as the time of their first interest. In the intervening years—during adolescence or college—the distributions are random.

An early interest in politics, especially if it develops in childhood, is likely to spring from a person's immediate interpersonal environment. The family is likely to stand out as the source of his "political socialization." As some of the interview material cited earlier indicates, some of the lawyers attributed their early interest in politics to parental influence. But do lawyers differ in this respect from non-lawyers? Table 3.2 suggests that they do. In each of the four states, greater proportions of the lawyer- than of the nonlawyer-legislators identified the family as an important agency of their political socialization. Some quotations from interviews with the lawyers will illustrate these figures.

Table 3.2
Perception of Family as Source of Political Socialization

	New Jersey		Ohio		Tennessee		California	
	L	NL	L	NL	L	NL	L	NL
Family perceived as active in or interested in politics	39%	29%	49%	34%	46%	30%	39%	25%
Number	41	38	59	103	39	81	33	80

I was brought up in it. My father was a leading political figure in the community. He was friends with all the leading political figures of the community. So, I really just grew up in and around politics.

My father was a member of the city council. He ran for Congress on the Republican ticket in 19—— and was defeated. I went to political meetings with him, I was always interested in politics. I heard him harangue about the tariff. I remember the election day which he spent with William Howard Taft, I therefore always felt a close identification with the Republican Party. On my mother's side the family was Democratic, her father was a Democratic candidate for ——. And my mother's mother was a suffragette, there was much discussion about women's franchise.

Well, it's sort of akin to law. After I was graduated from law school I was elected ward committeeman. My father previously had been a committeeman. I had an older brother who is a member of the school board in ——. He's an attorney too. We all are sort of involved in politics.

My grandfather was appointed a judge by McKinley and was a delegate to three or four national conventions. After him my father held public office as prosecuting attorney and was campaign speaker for the Republican Party for 30 years. In one campaign he campaigned in 28 counties and I went with him.

My father was in politics. When I was a kid he was prosecuting attorney. I was just raised on it. My grandfather was an attorney too and interested in politics though he never held office.

These perceptions are supported by more objective reports about "other members" of the family or "close relatives" who had held public or political office before the respondents themselves did. Although in California equal proportions of both lawyer- and non-lawyer-legislators reported that other family members and close relatives had been active, in the three other states, as Table 3.3 shows, more of the lawyers than of the nonlawyers did so.

Table 3.3
Family Members or Relatives Active in Politics

	New Jersey		*Ohio*		*Tennessee*		*California*	
	L	NL	L	NL	L	NL	L	NL
Family members or relatives in politics (one or more)	44%	37%	65%	55%	70%	54%	43%	43%
Number	41	38	59	103	39	81	33	80

If the particular offices held by legislators' family members or relatives are examined, no clear pattern emerges, but, as Table 3.4 indicates, some positions stand out. In the first place, in all four states relatives of lawyers held legislative positions at the state level more frequently than did the relatives of nonlawyers. Second, more of the lawyers' than of the nonlawyers' relatives held local judicial posts. And third, except in Ohio, more lawyers than nonlawyers had relatives or family members who had held party office or who had been active in political work.

The data support the notion of a "political family" that introduces its children into politics at an early age. Such early introduction into the political arena may, in some cases at least, lead to an intention to pursue a political career *before* the decision is made to enter law as an occupation most congenial to political activity. Present data do not permit us even to guess how common this chronological order-

Table 3.4
Political and Governmental Positions Held by Relatives*

	New Jersey		Ohio		Tennessee		California	
POSITION	L	NL	L	NL	L	NL	L	NL
Local executive	10%	11%	12%	13%	31%	30%	12%	6%
Local legislative	15	15	10	33	23	19	9	13
Local judicial	10	3	27	7	10	4	3	3
State executive	0	5	5	2	5	7	6	4
State legislative	12	8	19	9	33	19	15	10
State judicial	2	3	7	0	8	4	3	5
Federal executive	5	0	5	2	0	5	3	5
Federal legislative	2	3	5	1	0	1	6	3
Federal judicial	0	3	2	2	5	2	3	0
Party office/work	22	11	14	15	13	0	9	6
No office held	56	63	35	45	30	46	57	57
Other	0	0	0	0	3	0	0	0
Number	41	38	59	103	39	81	33	80

* Percentages total more than 100 because relatives could have held more than one office.

ing of orientations "from politics-to-law-to-politics" might be. But it is clearly a suggestive notion that deserves further exploration and illumination.

Apart from occupation, as the previous chapter noted, it is his higher educational attainment that distinguishes the lawyer from his nonlawyer colleagues in politics. But insofar as lawyers in politics attribute their political career to their legal education, the education factor merely confirms the compatibility of law and politics as professional pursuits. On the other hand, if other preprofessional educational experience is acknowledged as a source of political interest, this background, along with socialization in the milieu of the family, may well be an independent stimulus of the lawyer's political orientation—independent in the sense that it occurred prior to the future lawyer-politician's choice of a career.

Of course, it may be true that, precisely because they have a generally better and on the whole longer educational background than nonlawyers, lawyer-politicians will also be more disposed to recall pre-law-school educational experiences than will nonlawyers. This cannot be ascertained. But, regardless whether it is so or not, Table 3.5 shows that in all four states more of the lawyers than of the nonlawyers volunteered comments about educational experiences as

Table 3.5
Perception of Educational Experience as Source of Earliest Political Interest

	New Jersey		Ohio		Tennessee		California	
	L	NL	L	NL	L	NL	L	NL
Per Cent	15	3	19	12	18	4	27	16
Number	41	38	59	103	39	81	33	80

stimuli of early political interest. It is especially noteworthy that the interstate pattern evident in the table is not broken by California, where, in fact, both lawyers and nonlawyers report early educational experience in greater proportions than in the other three states. Apparently, the schools here serve as substitutive agents of political socialization, in place of the family. Some of the comments made in the interviews reveal the character of these educational influences:

> In high-school days I developed an interest in politics through reading good books, liking history—the appeal of being a statesman or politician (a term I don't like to use). As a kid I had a bad leg, couldn't participate in sports, and developed an interest in politics. I thought a legal background qualified a fellow for anything in public life. . . . In high school I thought of the study of law and the legislature for a career.

Primarily through reading. I enjoyed government classes, civics, and so on, particularly American history. I was pretty sure about pursuing this bent even when I was only a high-school sophomore.

I always liked it, even as a kid. The man who did the most and stimulated me the most was Dr. X, head of the government department at college. He was a Roosevelt New Dealer and I was a good Republican. We had some wonderful fights. I still drop in to see him whenever I'm down that way.

I've had an interest ever since I can remember. What set me off on the latest trend was in law school, a group of fellows who were all attempting to live on the GI Bill used to bring their lunches and eat in the seminar room, and we used to discuss politics. Finally we formed a Young Republican Club at the university and John W., who is the Attorney General, was one of the boys. The Young Republican Club joined the state organization and I became state chairman.

In general, the data suggest that lawyers come to politics at an earlier stage of their political life history than do nonlawyers. If all mentions of "long interest in politics" are inspected, as in Table 3.6, it appears that, except for a slight reversal of the pattern in Tennessee, more of the lawyers than of the nonlawyers give this highly general response.

Table 3.6
Perception of Long Interest in Politics

	New Jersey		Ohio		Tennessee		California	
	L	NL	L	NL	L	NL	L	NL
Per Cent	32	16	44	26	20	25	21	10
Number	41	38	59	103	39	81	33	80

A summary of all the comments that were made on early orientation to politics is helpful here. Table 3.7 reveals two especially suggestive types of distribution. First, lawyers in all four states consistently attributed their earliest interest in politics to primary social relations—with their family, relatives, or personal friends and associates—in greater proportions than did the nonlawyer-legislators.

Second, nonlawyers more than lawyers tended to give responses that, for lack of better terms, were classified under "particular events or conditions" and "personal predispositions." Although the patterns in each row are not wholly consistent from state to state, the differences are suggestive. The responses referred in many cases either to indulgent or to deprivational experiences—admiration for politicians, indignation with conditions—or to other stimuli either highly internal

Table 3.7
Major Sources of Political Interest*

SOURCE OF INTEREST	New Jersey		Ohio		Tennessee		California	
	L	NL	L	NL	L	NL	L	NL
Primary groups	54%	40%	53%	39%	46%	38%	48%	26%
Political or civic participation	58	60	51	47	44	43	79	65
Particular events or conditions	17	34	14	26	20	16	45	40
Personal pre-dispositions	49	58	49	50	33	32	45	54
Socio-economic beliefs	2	18	3	8	5	1	9	19
Not ascer-tained	0	0	5	9	3	7	3	6
Number	41	38	59	103	39	81	33	80

* Percentages total more than 100 because some respondents gave more than one answer.

(ambitions, obligation) or quite external (war, depression). It would seem that lawyers may not need to recall such early sources because they are initially better integrated than nonlawyers into the political structure by virtue of their abundant primary contacts with politically active or interested persons. But this is sheer speculation from data and not an interpretation of the data. On the other hand, whatever the case may be with nonlawyer-politicians, it is quite clear that the lawyer's political roots are not only deeper than the nonlawyer's but seem to be more firmly embedded in the whole network of political relations as well.

THE POLITICAL RECRUITMENT OF LAWYERS

Present data do not permit us to discriminate between those lawyer-legislators whose *cursus honorum* may have led from an early interest or even activity in politics to law as a profession, and those who, for whatever other reason, became lawyers first and then entered upon a career in politics. It was noted earlier that fewer of the lawyers than of the nonlawyers recalled first becoming interested in politics at the time of their entry into politics. This would seem to suggest—and anecdotal materials support the suggestion—that the lawyer's political career may have less of an accidental character than that of the nonlawyer, whose presence in politics may be a "fluke," and that it may be planned more "rationally" than the nonlawyer's.

In his study of American state governors, Schlesinger proposes and substantiates the fertile hypothesis that "the compatibility of the professions of law and politics operates to the advantage of lawyers primarily when they are career politicians."[3] In other words, Schlesinger suggests that the compatibility of law and politics as vocations may not be the same in every situation, but that it is dependent on the degree of an officeholder's *political* professionalization. Distinguishing between governors who had never held public office before becoming governor and those who had held prior office, Schlesinger found that lawyers did not predominate among the former—that, in other words, they did not enjoy a particular advantage that could be attributed to their being lawyers by profession. On the other hand, among those governors who had previously held

---

[3] Joseph A. Schlesinger, "Lawyers and American Politics: A Clarified View," *Midwest Journal of Political Science*, I (May 1957), 26.

public office, Schlesinger found that the greater the number of years they had spent in office, the greater was the number of lawyers among them. "This direct relation between the length of a man's career leading up to the governorship and his occupation," he concludes, "lends weight to the proposition that the lawyer in politics is to be equated with the careerist in politics."[4]

A political career pattern culminating in a governorship may, of course, be very different from a pattern that culminates, at least temporarily, in the state legislature. Findings true of governors need not be true of legislators. State legislative office is for most incumbents a part-time enterprise, whereas gubernatorial office is a full-time occupation. Few state legislators, as has been pointed out earlier, think of themselves as "careerists" in politics whether they are lawyers or not, even though they may not consider themselves "amateurs," however the term be defined.

Present data may shed some light on Schlesinger's hypothesis. Table 3.8 presents information concerning our respondents' pre-legislative governmental experience.

Table 3.8
Prelegislative Career—Level of Government

CAREER	New Jersey		Ohio		Tennessee		California	
	L	NL	L	NL	L	NL	L	NL
No previous experience	35%	34%	49%	39%	38%	57%	49%	45%
Local alone, or local and/or state, national	63	61	37	58	46	35	42	47
State and/or national	2	5	14	3	16	8	9	8
Total	100%	100%	100%	100%	100%	100%	100%	100%
Number	41	38	59	103	39	81	33	80

[4] *Ibid.*, p. 29.

As the table shows, only in Tennessee did the lawyer-legislators have prelegislative experience in greater proportion than the nonlawyers. In the other three states, nonlawyers had more governmental experience, but the differences are small. Most experience was had at the local level, but a few lawyers, in Ohio and Tennessee, had state or national experience. In general, it appears that, if previous governmental service is taken as an indicator, lawyer-legislators are not any more politically professionalized at the state legislative level than nonlawyer-politicians are. For many of these men the legislature was the first step into government service, and for many more it is probably the last step. As one lawyer respondent put it:

> Well, it's [i.e., the state legislature] the first step for a politician in politics. For me, it's probably the last step. As a Democrat, it was the only thing I could do. At the county level, although there are Democrats elected, all the incumbents were running again and I would not have had a good chance. There was more chance of success on the state level. You can learn more of the groundwork of politics here than anywhere else except the governorship.

On the other hand, a glance at Table 3.9 will show that, though substantial numbers of legislators in all four states had not held party office or been active in party political work before becoming state representatives, lawyers had been active in greater proportions than had nonlawyers. Only in Ohio was there almost no difference

Table 3.9
Prelegislative Career—Party Activity

	New Jersey		Ohio		Tennessee		California	
CAREER	L	NL	L	NL	L	NL	L	NL
No party office or work	38%	47%	63%	61%	55%	71%	36%	59%
Local/state/ national	62	53	37	39	45	29	64	41
Total	100%	100%	100%	100%	100%	100%	100%	100%
Number	41	38	59	103	39	81	33	80

between the two groups. But, without knowledge of the intensity of this involvement, it is hazardous to make any inferences from these data about political professionalism as a function of previous party activity.

The data concerning legislators' pre-office party activity are of interest in another respect. It is a not uncommon, though erroneous, assumption that a career in politics follows a regular series of steps—from party work at the local level to lesser local office, and from there to state or federal office. Yet, fairly large proportions of state legislators had never been active in their parties before being recruited into the legislature. Lawyers, it is true, were generally more active than nonlawyers, but does this mean that they planned a political career more purposefully than did nonlawyers? If they did, we should expect the parties' recruitment function to be more salient in lawyers' perceptions of their own political career.

Table 3.10
Perception of Agency of Recruitment*

	New Jersey		Ohio		Tennessee		California	
AGENCY	L	NL	L	NL	L	NL	L	NL
Political party	56%	66%	19%	20%	8%	15%	27%	19%
Self	34	21	51	55	23	14	36	26
Other	10	16	27	31	59	61	33	51
Not ascertained	12	8	7	1	33	26	3	9
Number	41	38	59	103	39	81	33	80

* Percentages total more than 100 because respondents could mention more than one agency of recruitment.

Recruitment of personnel into elective office is, in the American political system, one of the major functions performed by the parties. Yet, as Table 3.10 shows, on being asked how it happened that they became legislators, few respondents, except in New Jersey (where the parties are well organized and disciplined), pinpointed the parties as agencies of recruitment. More important, though the differences are small and the pattern is reversed in California, more of the nonlawyers than of the lawyers mentioned the parties in this connection.[5] This is surprising, because lawyers more than non-lawyers reported having been active in the parties.

Are these results due to inadequacies of the research, to deliberate falsification of the record by the respondents, or to the workings of chance? It would not seem so. Table 3.10 also shows that in all four states many legislators named themselves as the source or agency of their recruitment. One might readily write off this kind of response as self-serving and devoid of candor. But, except in Ohio, lawyers consistently name themselves more often as sponsors of their legis-lative career than do nonlawyers.[6] How is this to be interpreted, and how does it fill in the picture about recruitment?

It seems, and closer inspection of the interview protocols confirms, that though a respondent may be emphatic as regards the decision to become a legislator or politician having been his own, the party is usually lurking in the background as a recruitment agency. Analyze this response of a lawyer-legislator:

> Twenty years ago I developed the desire of becoming a legislator after practicing law a while. . . . Nobody told me to run. One of my associates is Democratic county chairman; he didn't know until I told him. . . . It was a long-planned thing. I was very active in club work, local politics, had extensive acquaintances. I was in a position to run and win.

This response is revealing in a number of respects. There is no doubt that the respondent considers himself a self-starter—"nobody told me to run." But, even if the decision is the respondent's own, it clearly takes place within the social context and cultural milieu of

---

[5] Similar results were obtained by David R. Derge in his study of the Indiana 1959 General Assembly, where only 24 per cent of the lawyers, but 35 per cent of the nonlawyers mentioned party leaders as important in their decision to seek legislative office. See "The Lawyer in the Indiana General Assembly," *Midwest Journal of Political Science*, VI (February 1962), 28, Table 4.

[6] The same was true in Derge's Indiana study, where 79 per cent of the lawyers but only 62 per cent of the nonlawyers gave this response. *Ibid.*

party politics: He is active in local politics and one of his associates is the party's county chairman. The most plausible interpretation would be that there is a subtle relationship of reciprocal influence between the individual and the party that is so taken for granted that the decision is really not made at all, at least not as a manifest decision. Just as the respondent can feel genuinely that the decision is his own and that the party is not involved, so the party (in this case through the chairman) does not have to make a determined, specific effort to recruit him as its candidate. There preexists an unspoken bond between potential recruit and the party as recruitment agency that makes the whole recruitment process appear "natural"—in the sense that neither side of the relationship is necessarily aware of its reciprocal character.

It is possible that other self-starters were in a similar position, though not many articulated the relationship equally well. But there is another aspect to this response that may explain why more of the lawyers than of the nonlawyers identify themselves as self-made politicians—"It was a long-planned thing. . . . I was in a position to run and win." Here the political career appears as rationally planned; and in this respect the lawyer, either by virtue of his earlier socialization into politics or by virtue of his legal training, is probably in a more advantageous position than the nonlawyer. Some quotations from interviews with lawyer-legislators will illustrate this further:

> Well, I had always thought that someday I would like to run for office; probably a legislative office. I think what really brought this to a head was that I served as a page in the Senate. After serving as a page I attended the Republican caucus in the spring of 19——. There was some discussion or comments made that perhaps a Republican should run against the incumbent. The incumbent was a solid Republican, but some people had gripes against him. I went to a member of the precinct committee, who was also vice-chairman of the party, and said I was interested in running. . . . I was no savior; I wanted the job. Logically I would have waited until I finished law school, but I felt the time was right. Even if I didn't win I would have campaign experience for the future. Things just seemed to

happen so that everything went smoothly. In my campaign I told the people I had wanted the job and that nobody asked me, I had asked them.

I could not say it was any one thing. In law school I was president of my class. I'm just interested to be part of the things that are happening and help influence how they happen. There were no particular circumstances. A good friend of mine was desirous to run and we discussed it. That made me think of it. I was also contacted by the Democratic Party and solicited to run. I had been recommended to them by the dean of the law school. But I had worked in campaigns for the Republicans and had contacts there. I solicited the nomination from the committee.

But the self-starting lawyer-politician, as the following quotation suggests, may also defy the party:

I did it just through campaigning. I had one endorsement, a local newspaper. I attribute a lot of my success to my father—since his name was well known. My dad was a Lausche Democrat. The county chairman and Lausche didn't see eye to eye. So I never solicited organization support. I just did it on my own. It was a lot of fun that way. They wouldn't let me speak at some meetings, but the harder they kicked me, the harder I tried. I am not a party politician . . . as yet.

The data, then, can be interpreted to support the notion that the lawyer is the prototype of the politician—no matter whether he lives for or off politics (in a professional sense rather than in Weber's economic sense). Just as the budding politician may follow Bryce's suggestion and purposefully decide on law as the vocation that best suits his political interest, so the man trained in law may purposefully plan a career in politics, for whatever reason, by laying the groundwork—joining clubs and associations, making wide acquaintances and friends, participating in local civic work, and perhaps entering party activity. Under these conditions he is likely to see himself as a self-starter, even if he plans his political career in the milieu of party politics.

Politicians, like other people, give "reasons" for what they do. These reasons may be effective springs of action. They may be indicative of candor or lack of candor, of genuine motivation or self-deception. Lawyers in particular, as members of a profession, should be expected to see "public service" in general, or service in behalf of a group or an ideal, as part of their political commitment. The long-standing conception of the lawyer as not simply his client's agent but also an "officer of the court" is indicative of a sense of public responsibility that has been part of the moral and intellectual tradition of the legal profession. And it does not matter whether the lawyer perceives such service as a means to his own personal advancement or not, in his public or in his private career.

It is to be expected, therefore, that in volunteering comments about how they became legislators, lawyers would be more likely than nonlawyers to articulate what, for lack of a better term, were coded as "altruistic-contributive" objectives of the legislative career—statements emphasizing public service, either in general or on behalf of specific groups. Yet, as Table 3.11 shows, this is not the case. In all four states, more of the nonlawyers gave these "altruistic-

Table 3.11
Major Types of Goals in Career Choice

	New Jersey		Ohio		Tennessee		California	
GOALS	L	NL	L	NL	L	NL	L	NL
Altruistic-contributive	20%	34%	32%	41%	15%	36%	33%	53%
Selfish-exploitative	15	10	24	13	36	16	18	24
Number	41	38	59	103	39	81	33	80

contributive" responses, and in three states, California being the exception, more of the lawyers gave "selfish-exploitative" responses. The pattern of responses may be indicative of a different style and stance that lawyers and nonlawyers bring to politics. Lawyers may be more candid than nonlawyers, more realistic and less stereotypic. Whatever the reason, some of the material in the interview protocols may serve to illustrate the kinds of "altruistic-contributive" response that are involved:

> I've been a worker in campaigns and have convictions, but I don't know that I'm a politician. I'm in it for my convictions. I felt going into politics would be beneficial and would give me an opportunity to serve. I naturally have a desire to make advances beneficial to my race [respondent is a Negro]. Money isn't everything and I'm not here for that. I want to make a contribution to this cause. . . . Whatever I can do to help will be my satisfaction, as is my reason for being in politics.

> I had always been interested in government. Perhaps it was due to the fact of an accumulation of experience in law and government. Also, I believe in conservatism in government and sought office to further this belief.

> I also was interested in maintaining the place of a person of the Jewish faith, there are so few of them in public life. . . . The man who held this position before me became a judge. He was of the Jewish faith also, the only one in the legislature. When he resigned, there was a vacancy. The head of the Republican Party was looking around and he suggested that I run. If I hadn't we would have lost the Jewish seat and we never would have been able to get it back.

THE POLITICAL ASPIRATIONS OF LAWYERS

Law has been traditionally a profession in which men from the "middle class" could rise higher in their own class and into the upper class. Of England in the late eighteenth and early nineteenth centuries, Elie Halevy has written, "a legal career was open to the ambition and the talents of the poorest, and led to the very highest positions in the society."[7] This, Bernard Barber has commented, "is a bit of an overstatement, since most social mobility through the law as elsewhere tended to be quite slow, consisting of relatively small

---

[7] Quoted in Bernard Barber, *Social Stratification* (New York: Harcourt, Brace and Company, 1957), p. 370.

rises upward."[8] In the United States, too, the legal historian James W. Hurst has stated, law has "a continuing role as one of the main roads of self-advancement for ambitious young men," especially those of lower-middle class in search of higher social status.[9] The law schools throughout the country, David Riesman has observed, "are still fairly wide open to 'talent,' irrespective of class, ethnic and kin lines. Thus, they attract the more ambitious, the more mobile young people. . . ."[10] It is only after he enters the profession, Riesman points out, that the young lawyer confronts class and ethnic barriers. Yet, the lawyer

> . . . takes social class and religion into account much less than is the case in many other professions (e.g., architecture). It is partly this that permits the law to remain one of the careers open to talent, so that a railroad conductor's son from Altoona, who has done well at a name law school, may end up as head of a big manufacturing or utility company, or a government agency, when he would never, without connections, have made the grade within the particular company or agency hierarchy.[11]

Today even those fortresses of legal conservatism, the Wall Street law firms, are crumbling. Before the Second World War, it is said, only the top students from Harvard, Yale, and a few other Eastern universities were hired by them, and Jews were excluded. Although discrimination is still practiced by some, today the demand for legal talent is so great that no firm can afford to pass up bright and ambitious young men, regardless of their origin or academic pedigree. Active recruitment programs are carried on at the better law

---

[8] *Ibid.*

[9] James Willard Hurst, *The Growth of American Law* (Boston: Little, Brown and Company, 1950), p. 254.

[10] David Riesman, "Toward an Anthropological Science of Law and the Legal Profession," in *Individualism Reconsidered* (New York: The Free Press of Glencoe, 1954), p. 452.

[11] *Ibid.*, pp. 454–455.

schools throughout the country.[12] Law not only attracts the ambitious and aspiring but also promises to satisfy their ambitions and aspirations.

Indeed, perhaps no other profession offers as many opportunities in a variety of directions. Some doctors may grow rich, but they do not generally become businessmen; some scientists may be called in as government advisers, but few become statesmen. Not so the lawyer. Though the popular image is probably still that of the solo practitioner who has learned enough about the mysteries of the law to be of help in personal injury suits, negligence claims, divorce actions, contract writing, and so on (an image by no means fictitious even today), the opportunities open to the modern lawyer may take him into lines that are often connected only remotely with what he may have learned in law school. Lawyers have made fortunes in business and have found fame in politics. The political career, in particular, promises ascendance to positions of great authority and power.

Just as the legal career may be oriented toward the achievement of higher status in the social structure, so may the political career facilitate political mobility. One need not necessarily assume that politicians are aspiring because they have personalities in whom power as a goal value is accentuated (under given conditions of motivation, skill, and opportunity).[13] It is sufficient to assume that, in the competitive environment of party or factional politics, politicians, and especially elective officeholders, will aspire to positions that are "higher" in the social scale of evaluation. As the American sociologist Edward A. Shils has written of Congressmen in another connection,

> In the United States politicians have an unusually high degree of social mobility. Politicians, more than any other profession, represent the realization of the idea of the poor boy who takes advantage of

---

[12] Erwin O. Smigel, "The Impact of Recruitment on the Organization of the Large Law Firm," *American Sociological Review*, XXV (February 1960), 55–66.

[13] See Harold D. Lasswell, *Power and Personality* (New York: W. W. Norton, 1948).

the opportunities of an open society and rises to the top. Even more
than businessmen and intellectuals, American politicians have moved
from the society of their birth and youth.[14]

Both law and politics, then, offer ambitious young men who are
appropriately inclined opportunities that in many respects are
parallel. In some jurisdictions, appointments to judgeships, whether
lucrative or not, are predicated on some form of political activity,
and judicial appointments are looked on as rewards for faithful party
service. Aspiring young lawyers who come to politics early and make
a political name for themselves clearly have an advantage over those
of their legal brethren who eschew politics. On the other hand, a
successful legal career and publicity gained in the legal career—and
this is particularly true of legal enforcement officers, such as district
attorneys—may bring the lawyer to the attention of the parties, forever on the lookout for "available" candidates whose private occupational achievements promise success at the polls.

Though law seems to be a profession open to talent irrespective
of social origin, it is a fact, nevertheless, that a great proportion of
lawyers come from families that are relatively high on any occupational status scale. A look at the social origins of state legislators,
measured, as in Table 3.12, by the occupational status of their
fathers, reveals that lawyer-legislators easily best their nonlawyer
colleagues in this respect. This, by the way, is true not only in the
four states considered in the present study but also in the states of
Indiana and Missouri, studied by David R. Derge.[15] On the other
hand, the differences between lawyers and nonlawyers should not
obscure the fact that in all these states a sizable minority of lawyer-
politicians comes from backgrounds with less highly valued parental
occupations—ranging from a low 15 per cent in Tennessee to a high
34 per cent in New Jersey.

Even though lawyer-legislators may come from occupationally
high-status families, this does not mean that they will be any

---

[14] Edward A. Shils, "The Legislator and his Environment," *University of
Chicago Law Review*, XVIII (Spring 1951), 581.

[15] See Derge, *op. cit.*, p. 21, Table 1.

Table 3.12
Status of Fathers' Occupations

FATHER'S OCCUPATION	New Jersey		Ohio		Tennessee		California	
	L	NL	L	NL	L	NL	L	NL
Professional	15%	21%	36%	13%	18%	12%	21%	18%
Managerial	41	26	22	22	36	28	37	29
Farmer, farm manager	5	8	12	36	31	43	6	24
All others	34	42	29	29	15	12	27	25
Not ascertained	5	3	1	0	0	5	9	4
Total	100%	100%	100%	100%	100%	100%	100%	100%
Number	41	38	59	103	39	81	33	80

less aspiring than their nonlawyer colleagues. As Harold Lasswell once put it, "middle-class homes are hothouses of ambition, holding their children to high standards of achievement, thus providing the tension between indulgence and deprivation so congenial to the accentuation of power."[16] The following extract from an interview illustrates how very close is the nexus between law and politics as mutually implicated careers in the perception of a lawyer-legislator of middle-class origin:

> I've always been interested in public affairs as long as I can remember. It's because of my family background. My father was interested in public affairs and my mother's family had many attorneys in public life. It's a family tradition. My great-grandfather . . . was attorney general and finally a member of the Senate, in other words, a big man in politics. *He was held up as a person worthy of being emulated.* It was always expected that in due course I would enter politics. I went to —— and wrote the executive charter which was passed. This was semi-public, and I achieved public recognition for it. This clinched my decision. . . . I came back from —— and I wanted to run for some office, either prosecutor or legislator. I talked

---

[16] Lasswell, *op. cit.*, p. 47.

it over with my father, and we decided that the state legislature was better because it would lead some place more than being the prosecutor of a small county. A prosecutor of a city might go some place, but a small county man isn't likely to go far: he usually ends up pleading property claims, and whereas I don't mind property claims, that isn't my ambition.

Others expressed similar sentiments in response to the question concerning the way in which they had become legislators. There is no reason to expect that lawyers and nonlawyers would differ in admitting to ambition, for both law and politics are appropriate careers for the ambitious. In all four states, lawyers consistently more than nonlawyers acknowledged their ambitions as reasons for seeking legislative office (Table 3.13).

Table 3.13
Expression of Ambition in Seeking Legislative Office

	New Jersey		Ohio		Tennessee		California	
	L	NL	L	NL	L	NL	L	NL
Per Cent	20	16	20	17	8	4	42	14
Number	41	38	59	103	39	81	33	80

The following two quotations from lawyer interviews illustrate these statements of ambition:

I guess it started with my getting interested in the study of civics in grade school and high school. I suppose this study of civics was my first inspiration. When I was working as a farmer and then as a railroad section hand *I wanted to better myself.* I then decided to go into law. What first prompted me was civics and what I learned about government. I am the only professional man in the whole family as far back as I've been able to trace.

That's hard to say. I would say that I'm sort of a person interested in doing things. I feel I should contribute from the policy point of view. I'm not a good joiner. I feel the same sort of thing carried over into government and politics. The same goes for policy-making. *I have always some desire not to be in the crowd.* I'm never content to go to meetings and just listen and go home. I like to get my oar in.

A political career, like a legal career, is a compound of motivation, skill, and opportunity. Though one more than another of these conditions for success may be critical in the case of a person who desires to advance in status, a quantity of each would seem to be a requisite, if in varying doses. State legislators were sensitive to the opportunity factor involved in their careers; and, as Table 3.14 shows, in all four states the lawyers seemed to be somewhat more sensitive to such circumstances than the nonlawyers. While the statements here coded as referring to "opportunity" were in part

Table 3.14
Perception of "Opportunity" as a Factor in Legislative Career

	New Jersey		Ohio		Tennessee		California	
	L	NL	L	NL	L	NL	L	NL
Per Cent	32	24	37	30	26	12	73	68
Number	41	38	59	103	39	81	33	80

quite general, those that were more specific suggest that by "opportunity" politicians mean those "breaks" which must be seized at the right time in the right place. Some excerpts from lawyers' interview protocols are relevant:

A vacancy came up and I had been building up toward it when the opening came. Then I made the move. All politics contains a certain amount of opportunity. If opportunities don't come, like anything else, you don't go any place. One has to be at the right spot at the right time. I happened to be.

Three years ago Mr. Y. gave a talk; I heard him, and told him that I would like to run for office some day. Mr. Y. followed it up the same year because it was a wide open race, and he thought I'd have a good chance. I wanted to finish law school first but you take opportunities as they come to you. I went back after the session, and finished school.

In 19—— the representative of my county resigned from his office, leaving a vacancy and allowing an open field. . . . Since I am from a traditionally and historically Democratic county, and since I am a

Republican, this let me gain office without opposing my predecessor. If this event hadn't happened I probably wouldn't have been a candidate at all. This is the major event that convinced me to go into it.

Of course, membership in the state legislature is hardly evidence of arrival at the top of the political ladder, and certainly not for the upwardly mobile. As the American political scientist Leon D. Epstein has observed,

> . . . legislative membership is part of the career pattern of some upwardly mobile individuals. Unlike those in congressional or other higher political positions, state legislators have not, by virtue of their office, reached either a highly remunerative or highly prestigious goal. But many may be on their way to such a goal, and if they are it is reasonable to expect some of the ambition to be reflected in an already established higher occupational status than that of their fathers.[17]

The data from the four states confirm Epstein's hunch. It appears that many legislators themselves perceive the state legislature as only a way station on the route to possibly "higher" office. In reply to the direct question as to whether or not they would like to seek other political or governmental positions, large proportions of respondents, lawyers as well as nonlawyers, answered either with a positive "yes" or with a more noncommittal "perhaps." As Table 3.15 shows, in three states—Ohio, Tennessee, and California—more of the lawyers than of the nonlawyers positively admitted to political aspirations beyond their present office. But even in New Jersey, if "yes" and "perhaps" answers are combined, slightly more of the lawyers than of the nonlawyers appear to be politically aspiring. For many New Jersey House members, as will appear in Table 3.16 (page 82), the state senate is an attractive next step, more attractive, indeed, than the federal Congress.[18] In general, it would seem that lawyers

---

[17] Leon D. Epstein, *Politics in Wisconsin* (Madison: University of Wisconsin Press, 1958), pp. 111–112.

[18] It should also be recalled that New Jersey lawyers had considerably higher incomes than lawyers elsewhere. With a lucrative private practice, political mobility appears to be less desirable, and lawyers seem to find political fulfillment at the state level, where they can continue in their practice.

Table 3.15

Political Aspirations Beyond the Legislature

	New Jersey		Ohio		Tennessee		California	
ASPIRATION	L	NL	L	NL	L	NL	L	NL
Yes	34%	47%	44%	30%	43%	21%	58%	29%
Perhaps	32	16	27	20	26	17	12	16
No	27	32	20	48	28	59	21	50
Not ascertained	7	5	9	2	3	3	9	5
Total	100%	100%	100%	100%	100%	100%	100%	100%
Number	41	38	59	103	39	81	33	80

more than nonlawyers are looking forward to another political office—evidence, perhaps, of their greater professionalization as politicians. This does not mean, of course, that all of them will make the grade, but it seems to explain, in part at least, why lawyers are found on "higher" levels of government even more frequently than nonlawyers are. Insofar as the state legislature serves as a proving ground for politicians, it appears that lawyers move on to other political offices not by predestination but by force of forethought.

This section has spoken of "other" office to which legislators might aspire, rather than of "higher" office. This has been quite deliberate, for "ranking" political or governmental positions in a federal system as complex as that of the United States presents an embarrassing problem, one that will not be solved here. However, attention should be called to it because, obviously, one cannot speak of "upward political mobility" without some fairly definite conception of just which office is "higher" or "lower" in a rank order of offices. There are probably two different, but not necessarily contradictory, answers. On the one hand, there probably exists enough intersubjective agreement that a United States Senator is "higher" on the political status scale than a state legislator or city councilman. On the other hand, whether being a United States Senator is preferable to being a municipal or state judge, for instance, or whether being a judge on any level is preferable to being the mayor of a metropolis, are questions on which there is likely to be little agreement. Here answers will depend not so much on a person's evaluation of offices as on his appraisal of his own skills and limitations in the professional division of labor. A lawyer-legislator may well think of "bettering" his station in life by becoming a municipal judge—an office in which his legal skills and interests are immediately relevant—rather than by becoming a federal congressman, and so on. The following two quotations concerning their political aspirations by lawyer-legislators are illustrative:

> The final result will be to get on the municipal court bench. The municipal court is the court through which 90 per cent of all the people come. They judge the whole system of jurisprudence through their experiences there. If the judge is good, and they have a good impression, then they like the whole system, but if they have a bad experience, then they are bitter.

> The counties are getting so big they'll have to consolidate many of their township departments under one county head. For example, all the sewerage and water supply departments will have to come under one county commissioner. I'd like to run for this position.

For the first respondent, then, the municipal bench, and for the second, a county administrative department, is a desirable goal of a political career. Of course, lawyer-legislators, in contrast to non-lawyers, have one option—the judiciary—that simply is not available to all politicians. Table 3.16 presents the levels and types of office that respondents named as goals of their political career aspirations. As the distributions show, only a handful of nonlawyers mentioned judicial office on the local level, and not a single one named judicial office on the state level, a fact indicative of the legal profession's monopoly of the judiciary. What is interesting, from the perspective of rank-ordering such offices, is that in two states, Ohio and Tennessee, more lawyers evidently considered local judicial office preferable to state judicial office, and that only one lawyer aspired to the federal bench. Quite apart from the ranking problem, however, the data suggest that these statements of aspiration reflect a good deal of

Table 3.16
Lawyers' and Nonlawyers' Level of Aspirations*

LEVEL AND TYPE OF OFFICE	New Jersey		Ohio		Tennessee		California	
	L	NL	L	NL	L	NL	L	NL
Local executive	0%	5%	2%	4%	8%	7%	0%	3%
Local legislative	0	13	3	1	0	1	0	5
Local judicial	5	0	24	1	10	5	0	0
State executive	10	11	0	7	10	1	12	11
State legislative (other House)	29	11	8	7	18	10	15	6
State judicial	8	0	3	0	5	0	21	0
Federal executive	0	5	0	1	0	0	3	0
Federal legislative	12	26	32	30	26	10	25	19
Federal judicial	0	0	2	0	0	0	0	0
Other**	7	5	2	4	8	11	6	4
Not ascertained	42	40	36	56	39	62	33	62
Number	41	38	59	103	39	81	33	80

* Percentages total more than 100 because more than one office could be mentioned.

** Respondents mention office but not level, or level but not office.

political realism—the number of state and federal judicial posts is limited and only a few reach them.

Moreover, judicial appointment or election, on any level, may be viewed not as a further step in a *political* career but as a terminus. In this regard, then, lawyer-politicians who aspire to executive or other legislative positions may qualitatively differ from those who would like to fill a judicial office. This hypothesis cannot be pursued in detail here, but it is to be expected that lawyer-legislators who see judicial office as the culmination of their political career are those who came to law first and then picked up politics, whereas lawyer-legislators seeking nonjudicial positions might be expected to have been politically oriented first and then to have chosen law as the vocation best suited to their political ambitions. Whatever the case may be, Table 3.16 shows that more lawyer-legislators seem to aspire to another legislative office than to judicial office, suggesting that, perhaps, the particular type of lawyer involved in this study is in fact a politician first and a lawyer second.

Lawyers' comments in connection with the question about their political career aspirations may convey some of the considerations that seem to enter into the decision to seek other office; in particular, the emphasis on the "opportunity" factor is again noteworthy:

> There's one thing in politics—you have to take advantage of op-portunities. The timing is important. But unless you have much money or backing you have difficulty to make your own opportunity.

> I wouldn't say that there aren't and I wouldn't say that there are [other positions that respondent might seek]. As you may have surmised, my theory is that you should be able to take politics or leave it alone. I don't mean just financially. You should have an-other life, a means of livelihood, so it isn't your whole soul.

> I'd like to run for Congress. Will stay here until the time is ripe. The difficulty is that I'm a Republican from a Democratic Congres-sional district. It will be difficult to win. I have to wait for the right time, and the right opposition. Maybe next year. If I were a Democrat I could win now, I think.

> . . . The situation is important. The Congressional Representative from my county is not well. He can beat any opponent; he is clever but conservative. There are at least half a dozen people looking for that job. There is nothing in particular that I have an eye on. ["What are your aspirations?"] You mean my pipe dream? U.S. Senator. I think that's about the nicest job around in politics. But again every-thing depends on the situation. For example, if I want to consider the welfare of my law practice, it would be best for me to stay right here.

When you have an interest in government, you would like to assume positions where you can take a heavier load. I would, of course, like a Congressional job. Everyone would. You make $25,000; this would probably be the main reason I'd be interested in it.

Well, every fellow in political life finds himself moving in some direction. I have no conscious goal, but I might be interested in being on the bench or in some other judicial capacity. It's not a burning desire. A fellow has to be fatalistic about this. If it works out it does, and if not it doesn't.

National Congress. However, my law practice can continue while I am in the state legislature. When I run for a state office or Congress, I am really *out* of law and *in* politics.

Of course, the data do not tell us whether the state legislature is, in fact, a good stepping stone for judicial office on whatever level, for executive office, or for Congress. Matthews reports that of the 180 senators who sat between 1947 and 1957, 21 per cent had held state legislative as their *first* political office, but that only about ten per cent had been in the state legislature immediately before entering the Senate.[19] No similar information is readily available for the House of Representatives. Of 841 state governors between 1870 and 1950, according to Schlesinger, 200, or 24 per cent, had held state legislative office prior to their gubernatorial election. Of these, 39 per cent were lawyers by profession.[20] Of 23 major-party presidential nominees between 1832 and 1892, 57 per cent had previously served, at one time or another, in a state legislature. But the proportion declined to 24 per cent for the 17 nominees between 1896 and 1956. "The state legislatures," comment David, Goldman, and Bain, "like some phases of local government, provide relatively easy beginning points for some types of political careers, but presidential careers

---

[19] Donald R. Matthews, *U.S. Senators and Their World* (Chapel Hill: University of North Carolina Press, 1960), pp. 51, 56.

[20] Schlesinger, *op. cit.*, p. 33, Table 3.

seldom begin there."[21] Of 90 Supreme Court justices appointed between 1789 and 1957 who had previously held political positions, only 6.6 per cent had been in state legislative office as the "highest political post" prior to their appointment.[22] State legislative office is certainly not a necessary way station for mobile politicians. In some cases it may serve as a proving ground or even as a takeoff point for a political career.

This chapter has proceeded from the assumption that the lawyer's political career, like his legal career, is vocational—that he feels almost compulsively called on to pursue one as he pursues the other. This assumption is useful because it calls attention to those aspects of the political career that should help to discriminate between the political professional and the amateur. It is, of course, an assumption relevant only to lawyers in politics. There are many more lawyers who never participate in party politics or seek governmental office either as professionals or as amateurs than there are lawyers who are politically active. And even among the active there are many who do not look upon their work in politics or government as anything but an avocation. However, lawyer-legislators who are in politics only as a hobby cannot be isolated from the whole group. It cannot be assumed, therefore, that those who plan to leave the legislature or do not aspire to another office are of this type. But some comments made by those lawyers who specifically volunteered remarks about their primary commitment to law rather than to politics as a profession can be cited:

> *Politics is a sideline for me*, since I'm a lawyer by profession. When I first came back from the army I was approached by a group to run for office. I won the primary and I won the general election. I have

---

[21] Paul T. David, Ralph M. Goldman, and Richard C. Bain, *The Politics of National Party Conventions* (Washington, D.C.: The Brookings Institution, 1960), p. 147. For the data cited here, see p. 148, Table 7.10. For data on other presidential and on vice-presidential contenders, see pp. 147-153.

[22] John R. Schmidhauser, "The Justices of the Supreme Court: A Collective Portrait," *Midwest Journal of Political Science*, III (February 1959), 37, Table 12.

been able to accomplish some of the things I wanted to do in the legislature, and it is a satisfying feeling.

I would say that I was catapulted into politics without any approach. My law partner was ———, who at the time of his death was ———. He had been city councilman here in ——— and had held other political jobs. So I had naturally worked in his behalf in these campaigns. . . . This I did for a number of years. So from there I was asked to run for the legislature. *I did not seek the job, I was asked.*

My service is here for now. But what the future will hold I can't say. I would say that I would want to stay in political life, as it would fit into my legal practice. *I am primarily a lawyer.*

CONCLUSION

Comparison of the political careers of lawyer- and non-lawyer-legislators suggests one tentative hypothesis: that differences in career patterns between them may be due less to lawyers' legal training than to the possibility that many lawyers may begin to participate in politics before they embark on a legal career. If this is so, it goes a long way toward explaining the ubiquity of lawyers in politics and toward explaining why the lawyer-politician seems to be more "politicized" than the politician who is not a lawyer.

Chapter 4

THE ROLE CLUSTER

The lawyer's manifold roles stem from expectations concerning his function and conduct held by at least three sets of "significant others"—his clients, his colleagues of bar and bench, and the larger society in which he lives. As Blaustein and Porter somewhat dramatically put it,

> . . . the lawyer faces and must resolve the conflicting loyalties he owes to his three masters—the client, the court, and society. In a very real sense the attorney is confronted with ethical problems greater than those of any other profession. The minister owes his obligation only to God, and the physician only to his patient (with some statutory exceptions). But the lawyer must decide whether the steps he should take, in serving a particular client, will also serve the best interests of the judicial branch of government and of society as a whole.[1]

The authors of this paragraph are only partly right. Ministers and physicians, too, serve "three masters." And so do politicians. Compare the above paragraph with the following extract from an interview with a lawyer-legislator in one of the four states of this study:

> A legislator has a three-way responsibility—to his constituents, to the state of ——— as a whole, and to the general assembly as a body. A legislature is designed to pass laws, and no one person can have his way on everything. Most of the legislation is composed of compromise

---

[1] Albert P. Blaustein and Charles O. Porter, *The American Lawyer* (Chicago: University of Chicago Press, 1954), p. 44.

measures. If you voted "no" on every bill you didn't understand, not much would be passed. Legislation depends on judgments whether a bill is good or bad. Lots of legislation is passed on the faith of what others say.

This study's concern is not in examining the conflict potential inherent in the lawyer's roles as he confronts his obligations to clients, colleagues, and the public at large, or in the politician's roles as he faces his constituents, his peers, or the larger community. Nor is the way in which role conflict is avoided or reduced our focus. But if a cluster of roles involves a variety of expectations and attendant obligations, either the division of labor tends to make for the segmentalization of the cluster, so that its component roles may be taken by different persons;[2] or the actor himself may develop such great versatility in adapting to different expectations that he can mobilize whatever component of the multi-functional central role he is expected to take in a variety of circumstances.[3]

The affinity of law and politics suggests that lawyers should not be expected to differ from nonlawyers in the taking of those roles that are typically associated with the central role of "legislator." This chapter will review at least some of the roles arising from the lawyer's social interactions with clients, colleagues, and the public at large. It will also examine, both theoretically and empirically, just how lawyers and nonlawyers may be similar or different in assuming some of the roles that, in the larger project from which present data come, were identified as particularly characteristic of the modern legislator. In this connection it is well to recall that this study deals with respondents' own definitions of their legislative roles—their role orientations—rather than with the expectations of others with

[2] See John C. Wahlke and others, "The Concept of Role and the Model of the Legislative Actor," in *The Legislative System* (New York: John Wiley & Sons, 1962), pp. 7–17.

[3] "In sociological terminology, a profession is a cluster of 'occupational' roles, that is, roles in which the incumbents perform certain functions valued in the society in general. . . ." Talcott Parsons, "A Sociologist Looks at the Legal Profession," in *Essays in Sociological Theory* (New York: The Free Press of Glencoe, 1954), p. 372.

whom legislators interact in the performance of their legislative functions.

THE CLIENT RELATIONSHIP: STYLE

At the heart of the lawyer's cluster of roles is the role that relates him to his clients. This relationship has long been acknowledged as one of "trust," in the sense that communications between the lawyer and his client are fiduciary and confidential. These communications must not be made public even if the lawyer's own interest or the public interest might require it. In order to meet the requirement of confidence involved in his trusteeship role vis-à-vis clients, the lawyer must be independent of outside pressures that would deny him the possibility of appraising his client's problem independently, whether it is "legal" or not, and that would oblige him to reveal the nature of private transactions between him and his client.

But the lawyer's independence has another aspect as well: He is, in some respects, independent of his client also. He is expected to be primarily interested in the client's *case* rather than in the client as a person or, as increasingly happens, a corporation or business, an association, a union, or a government bureau. This serves to protect him, as Talcott Parsons has pointed out, "in that he is enabled to participate in private affairs without himself becoming too deeply involved, either in judgment of the legality of the client's position, or in responsibilities to his client going too far beyond their professional relationship."[4] A lawyer may withdraw from a case if he feels that a client ignores these obligations and makes demands of a personal nature that the lawyer does not recognize as legitimate aspects of the relationship.

Like the lawyer, the modern legislator has a variety of "clienteles" —most obviously his district and its residents, but also collective actors on the political scene, such as parties, pressure groups, and ad-

---

[4] *Ibid.*, p. 381.

ministrative agencies. All these clienteles entertain expectations as to what the legislator as an elective officeholder and "representative" should do for them, what services they can legitimately demand of him, and so on. The *content* of these expectations and demands, giving rise to the legislator's "focal" roles, is not of immediate interest here. Of relevance is the "style" of representation the legislator may adopt in relating himself to the various clienteles that compete for his attention and services.[5]

Among the "representational roles" the legislator may take, three alternatives of style seem to be available to him. As a trustee, he will insist that in his decision-making behavior he should be left free to reach an independent judgment—independent, that is, from his clienteles—on the basis of his principles and convictions, or on the basis of his appraisal of the facts. As a delegate, the legislator feels obliged to follow whatever mandate or instructions may be given him by his clienteles, or he acknowledges at least a strong dependence on them for advice and suggestions as to how he should conduct himself in his decision-making. Finally, the legislator may take a stylistic-representational role which, for lack of a better term, is called "politico." The role of politico is based on the assumption that the roles of trustee and delegate, though theoretically mutually exclusive, are not mutually antagonistic in empirical reality. As a politico, the legislator may adopt one role or the other as circumstances require, or he may even try to reconcile them in a single action. The normative question, which of these roles—trustee or delegate—is "right and proper," has, of course, been at the core of the many controversies over the "nature" of representation that have arisen in the history of political philosophy.[6]

Of the three representational roles that express the legislator's style in his relationships with his clienteles, that of trustee is evi-

---

[5] For discussion and discrimination between style and focus of representation, see Wahlke, *op. cit.*, pp. 269–272.

[6] See Heinz Eulau, John C. Wahlke, William Buchanan, and LeRoy C. Ferguson, "The Role of the Representative: Some Empirical Observations on the Theory of Edmund Burke," *American Political Science Review*, LIII (September 1959), 742–756.

dently more or less equivalent to the lawyer's traditional conception of his fiduciary role vis-à-vis his clients. That both lawyers and non-lawyers find this role congenial is clearly evident in Table 4.1. Lawyer- as well as nonlawyer-legislators take the role of trustee in greater proportions than any other representational role. That in Ohio fewer of the lawyers than of the nonlawyers take the trustee

Table 4.1

Representational Roles of Lawyers and Nonlawyers

REPRESENTA- TIONAL ROLE	New Jersey		Ohio		Tennessee		California	
	L	NL	L	NL	L	NL	L	NL
Trustee	42%	40%	34%	43%	51%	53%	33%	20%
Delegate	7	18	5	14	5	4	9	9
Politico	15	16	30	15	8	9	6	13
Other	10	13	10	9	3	6	9	14
Not ascertained	26	13	21	19	33	28	43	44
Total	100%	100%	100%	100%	100%	100%	100%	100%
Number	41	38	59	103	39	81	33	80

role seems to result largely from the fact that lawyers there also take in fairly large proportions the much more complex role of politico, with its "built-in" trustee dimension. In other words, Ohio differs much less from the other states than seems to be the case at first glance, and we cannot assume that lawyers there are any less "trusteeish" than nonlawyers. In California, the apparently lower proportions of trustees among both lawyers and nonlawyers are probably an artifact of the greater proportions of nonrespondents. Some extracts from the interview protocols will illustrate lawyers' interpretations of the political trustee role:

> I operate on the principle that I'm here to use my own judgment. A representative is good as long as his ideas coincide with the con- stituents' wishes. If they don't, it's up to them to throw me out, not for me to change. Not that I don't think you should listen to them. Still, I think a legislator should do what he thinks best regardless of public opinion. I do pretty much what I think is best. I operate on the

idea that the sooner I get tossed out and go back to law practice the better off I'll be. You see guys who follow the whims of the people. What's wrong with that is that they're not smart enough to figure out what the people think. Hell, it's hard enough to decide what you think.

The most important job is to gain an understanding of the real problems of the state and an ability to reach decisions to solve them without being unduly influenced by the feelings of persons who are committed or paid, or people who for lack of information or ability are incapable of reaching a decision. I do not consider myself as a delegate. People are not capable to tell me what to do—not because they are stupid, but because they have limited access to the facts. If they had the facts, their decision would be the same.

His most important and difficult job is to vote according to his conscience without letting other things interfere—even your own constituents. They are ax-grinding elements. Listen to them, but follow your conscience and let the chips fall where they may. I'm one of the best in politics, have never been defeated. Some are afraid to get defeated; they are dead wrong. My creed: I vote my conscience in what to do on a bill.

As these quotations indicate, the trustee role springs from two sources: the legislator's perception of his clients as whimsical, ill-informed, or ax-grinding; and the legislator's perception of himself as a man who is responsible for his own action, has access to the facts, or is a servant of his own conscience. These perceptions are, in many respects, the lawyer's perceptions of his clients and of himself as a lawyer. If, as is sometimes argued, lawyer-legislators were retained by clients to advance their interests in the legislature, lawyers should be expected to take the delegate role rather than the trustee role, and in greater proportions than the nonlawyers. Yet, as Table 4.1 shows, this is not the case. It may well be that lawyers are more adept in concealing such retainer relations (where the line between influence and corruption is hard to draw), but the impression which reviewing the interview protocols from four legislatures gives is that, whether or not this may have been the case in the past, it is rarely the case today. Rather, as the politico role suggests, legislators are candid about the problem of reconciling their commitments and are even prepared, as the first of the following comments indicates, to discuss frankly the problem of "conflict of interest":

> It is a hard job to represent such varied interests. One important thing is the problem of conflict of interest. Most members of the legislature are engaged in private occupations, and at times this gives rise to situations where private endeavor and public duty are in conflict. Even though an individual may resolve the conflict in his own mind, since there is no law or precedent defining the problem, the individual legislator can be attacked for his stand by groups' or newspapers' ideas of what constitutes conflict of interest. Steps should be taken to clarify the position of the legislator with respect to any private interests that he may have. This may result in setting standards that will exclude some people because of limitations on income and may make it necessary to consider higher salaries to get people of high caliber to serve.

> It's very hard to say [what the job of legislator is]. I've occupied a number of positions. In each position you try to . . . well, that gets you into a major philosophical question. Is it the duty of the representative simply to do what people want, or is it his duty to figure out what's in the best interest of people and state, and persuade them that it is? Uniformly, I have not taken either position—sometimes one, sometimes the other. Sometimes I've flown in the face of overwhelming sentiment and tried to show them why they should not take the stand they were taking. The evidence of success is that I'm still here.

> As I see the legislature . . . the basic job is to act as an agent of the people's will in the political sense of the word. It isn't exactly the job of being the Gallup Poll kind of thing, but in writing the laws and making them appropriate. Setting policies, setting the balance between what the constituents want and what our own judgments tell us. That's why not anyone can be a legislator. Striking a balance is hard. A person has to be sensitive to pressures and also be independent of them. There's no easy way to say where you start and stop.

THE CLIENT RELATIONSHIP: FOCUS AND SCOPE

It is symptomatic of the multifaceted focus and scope of the lawyer's total professional role that "advocate," "attorney," and "counselor" are used interchangeably to describe what the lawyer does or is expected to do. Yet, if literally interpreted, each denotes quite different aspects of the total role, and each refers to quite different, if interrelated, functions involved in the lawyer's business vis-à-vis his clients.

Advocate

The lawyer is traditionally an advocate—a pleader in court for his client's side in a legal controversy. As advocate, the lawyer is typically engaged after some problem has arisen that needs legal intervention and seems to depend on legal controversy as the only solution. His job is to "build up" his case and present it in a way that favors his client's position. Before 1870, writes the legal historian James Willard Hurst,

> . . . both in their own eyes and in the opinion of laymen, lawyers' distinctive business was contest in court; the criterion in handling most matters out of court was how the arrangement would stand up under a later challenge in court; by common consent in the typical community the prices in reputation, public influence, and wealth were the due of the able advocate.[7]

His knowledge of the law and forensic skills presumably make the lawyer a persuader par excellence. Court procedure institutionalizes an adversary system—a system that, as the German sociologist Georg Simmel has pointed out, is "absolute":

> That is, on both sides the claims are put through with pure objectivity and with all means that are permitted; the conflict is not deflected or attenuated by any personal or in any other sense extraneous circumstances. Legal conflict is pure conflict in as much as nothing enters its whole action which does not belong to the conflict *as such* and serves its purpose. . . .
>
> This elimination of all that is not conflict can of course lead to a formalism which becomes independent of all contents. On the one

---

[7] James Willard Hurst, *The Growth of American Law* (Boston: Little, Brown and Company, 1950), p. 302.

hand, we here have legal pettifoggery. In legal pettifoggery, it is not objective points which are weighed against one another; instead, concepts lead an entirely abstract fight. On the other hand, the conflict is sometimes delegated to agents which have no relation to what their contest is to decide. The fact that in higher cultures, legal quarrels are carried out by professional counsels, certainly serves the clean separation of the controversy from all personal associations which have nothing to do with it. . . .[8]

Political conflict can hardly be said to be "pure conflict" in Simmel's ideal-type legal sense. Yet, the political arena, like the legal arena, is one of conflict. As the lawyers are the combatants in the sphere of law, so politicians are the contenders in the sphere of politics. Max Weber, trying to explain the prominence of lawyers in politics since the rise of political parties, noted the functional similarity of party conflict and legal conflict:

> The management of politics through parties simply means management through interest groups. . . . The craft of the trained lawyer is to plead effectively the cause of interested clients. . . . [An official] can advocate and win a cause supported by logically weak arguments and one which, in this sense, is a "weak" cause. Yet he wins it because technically he makes a "strong case" for it. But only the lawyer successfully pleads a cause that can be supported by logically strong arguments, thus handling a "good" cause "well." All too often the civil servant as a politician turns a cause that is good in every sense into a "weak" cause, through technically "weak" pleading. . . . To an outstanding degree, politics today is in fact conducted in public by means of the spoken or written word. To weigh the effect of the word properly falls within the range of the lawyer's tasks. . . .
>
> To take a stand, to be passionate—*ira et studium*—is the politician's element, and above all the element of the political leader.[9]

---

[8] Georg Simmel, *Conflict* (New York: The Free Press of Glencoe, 1955), pp. 36–37.

[9] Max Weber, "Politics as a Vocation," in H. H. Gerth and C. Wright Mills, *From Max Weber: Essays in Sociology* (New York: Oxford University Press, 1946), pp. 94–95. James Bryce, too, noted the advocacy component of both law and politics: The legal profession's "action in political life may be compared with its function in judicial proceedings. Advocacy is at the service of the just and unjust equally." *The American Commonwealth* (rev. ed., New York: The Macmillan Company, 1911), II, 307.

Of the roles that were identified in the original project as pe-
culiarly characteristic of advocacy, one was characterized as
"tribune." The tribune is the people's advocate in the political do-
main. The role is historically rooted in the representative's function
to fight the people's battle against the Crown, and it finds modern
expression in statements to the effect that the legislator is a defender
of popular interests and an advocate of popular demands. The
lawyer as advocate and the politician as tribune are roles that seem
to be functionally equivalent.[10] Some examples from the interviews
may illustrate the latter role:

> We try to meet the demands of the people, and to solve the prob-
> lems put in front of us. . . . [The legislator] has to have vision and
> fortitude. He must do the most good for the most people, and pass
> legislation which helps the state toward progress. In that way, he can
> benefit the people.

> The most important job is to make a study of all the departments
> of government and study the laws applicable to those departments
> and the methods of financing state government without extravagance.
> There's so much waste here that I see now that I didn't see before.
> Do you see all these bound notebooks and journals here? This print-
> ing and binding costs thousands of dollars which could be used by
> the legislature for people who have needs like mental health. The
> good legislator gives time to someone who is in need. Some industries
> and businesses have lobbyists to keep us informed about what they
> want. But other groups that may be needy don't even know how to
> organize. They need help too.

> Most important is to understand people. You have to learn to
> differentiate between the real voice of the people and pressure
> groups. You must be sincere. You will have to work long hours. You
> must be pretty unselfish about it because most of the things you
> really accomplish very few know or care about.

Table 4.2 shows the proportions of lawyers and nonlawyers who
articulated the role orientation of the tribune. Although in all four
states nonlawyers were somewhat more inclined than lawyers to

---

[10] For fuller discussion of the tribune role, see Wahlke, *op. cit.*, pp. 247–248
and 252–254.

Table 4.2
Tribune Role of Lawyers and Nonlawyers

	New Jersey		Ohio		Tennessee		California	
	L	NL	L	NL	L	NL	L	NL
Per Cent	61	66	36	42	49	62	52	56
Number	41	38	59	103	39	81	33	80

subscribe to this orientation as an important component of their total legislative role, nowhere, except perhaps in Tennessee, is the difference in proportions in any way startling. If lawyers still find the tribune role congenial, they do not seem to find it more congenial than do other elective politicians. Though courtroom advocacy and brief-making remain important functions of the legal profession, the lawyer's other functions—negotiation outside the courtroom or advice-giving, for instance—have come to be increasingly central as far as the legal profession is concerned.

The tribune orientation does not tell us anything about its holder's intensity as an advocate. David Riesman has pointed out that "it is frequently said that lawyers are particularly partisan people; this is part of the stereotype. . . . Yet it is a question if lawyers are more opinionated than most people; they are ordinarily less partisan than nonlawyers and could hardly do their work if this were not so."[11] But, Riesman continues, "there are other times when the client cannot tolerate a nonpartisanship which is clearly in his own interest. . . . The demand for partisanship comes, moreover, not only from the client, but from the lawyer's own desire to believe in the client as a cause."[12]

When speaking of partisanship, we are of course speaking of an attitude, not of a role. But partisanship is likely to be affected by the "collective roles" that parties play in the total configuration of a

---

[11] David Riesman, "Toward an Anthropological Science of Law and the Legal Profession," in *Individualism Reconsidered* (New York: The Free Press of Glencoe, 1954), p. 457.

[12] *Ibid.*, p. 458.

political system. Table 4.3 presents some relevant results.[13] In the first place, note that, in the competitive two-party systems of New Jersey and Ohio, majorities of legislators exhibit a partisanship stance, but lawyers are more partisan than nonlawyers. However, they differ clearly in the proportions who are weak partisans. In two-party systems, it seems, lawyers may be more committed to their parties than nonlawyers—not an unlikely result in view of the fact that the parties in these systems are the main routes of political mobility for the politically aspiring; and since lawyers, as was noted

Table 4.3
Party Partisanship of Lawyers and Nonlawyers

DEGREE OF PARTISANSHIP	New Jersey		Ohio		Tennessee		California	
	L	NL	L	NL	L	NL	L	NL
More	93%	82%	91%	73%	57%	46%	69%	45%
Less	7	18	7	25	35	47	24	52
Not ascertained	0	0	2	2	8	7	7	3
Total	100%	100%	100%	100%	100%	100%	100%	100%
Number	41	38	59	103	39	81	33	80

in the chapter on careers, are probably more "politicized" than other politicians, they should be expected to be more devoted to the parties as the most readily available avenues of political ascent. In Tennessee, with its weak party and strong factional system, fewer legislators than in New Jersey and Ohio are partisan, but lawyers are again somewhat more partisan than nonlawyers. In California, finally, with a party system in transition in 1957, note the much greater proportions of partisan lawyers. This suggests that perhaps lawyers may have been in the forefront of those intent on making the state's politics move in the direction of a more clear-cut party system. In general, then, it would seem that lawyers do, at least as

---

[13] For construction of the partisanship index, see Appendix, p. 153.

far as the parties are concerned, assume partisan attitudes more than nonlawyers do, possibly because they see more clearly the advantage partisanship affords in a viable two-party system.

Attorney

The modern lawyer often is not so much an "advocate" or "pleader" as a negotiator, mediator, or arbitrator. Before the growth of commerce and land speculation in the mid-eighteenth century, "law business was apparently done mainly by 'attorneys' who were in fact laymen under no professional discipline, who depended chiefly on shrewdness with tongue or pen to qualify to speak for others in court and attend to their affairs outside it."[14] In his role of "attorney" the lawyer is presumably an agent appointed to transact his client's business; but he is also free to do so by ways and means that need not involve judicial proceedings, whether or not the business at hand involves conflictual or contractual matters. "Settlement out of court" is often considered preferable to costly and drawn-out legal proceedings. As lawyers have less personal involvement in the "case" than do their principals, they are in a particularly advantageous position to negotiate with each other. Although exact information concerning the proportion of the lawyer's work load that involves legal advocacy and the proportion that calls for negotiation or mediation is difficult to come by, it is now generally felt that the lawyer is more attorney than advocate.

Like attorneys, politicians, especially in highly pluralist societies, are "go-betweens." Skill in compromising and bargaining is the mark of the successful politician who survives the strains and tensions of the manifold, often contradictory demands that are made on him.[15] The function of the lawyer, as of the politician, as Robert E. Agger has suggested, is "to provide the element of flexibility and the

---

[14] Hurst, *op. cit.*, p. 253.

[15] Perhaps the best statement of the function of politics in a democratic, pluralistic order is still E. Pendleton Herring, *The Politics of Democracy* (New York: Rinehart & Company, 1940).

attitude of compromise necessary to multi-group politics."[16] In this respect, the lawyer as attorney and the politician as compromiser are not so much advocates and partisans involved in conflict as they are engineers of the society's fundamental consensus. "As guardians of 'the law' and justice," writes Agger, "lawyers when involved in politics tend to think of themselves as representing the 'community' or 'everyone' rather than business, agriculture or labor."[17] As both are specialists in the accommodation of interests and in the adjustment of conflicting demands, the roles of the lawyer and of the politician may be considered functionally equivalent.

The politician can relate himself to the gamut of interest- or pressure-groups in a variety of ways. In our original project, three role orientations pertinent to the struggle of groups in the legislature were constructed. As "facilitator" the legislator promotes the solution of intergroup conflict; as "resister" he opposes group demands; and as "neutral" he is rather indifferent to pressure politics.[18] It should be emphasized that these role orientations do not tell us, implicitly or explicitly, just what particular groups the legislator may favor or oppose, or what groups may or may not have direct access to his services. Rather, these orientations tap a general disposition to take a role that is relevant to the relations existing between the legislature as an institution and the interest groups active in it. Our interest here is, of course, in the legislator's role of facilitator, which seems to be the functional equivalent of the lawyer's role as mediator or negotiator.

Table 4.4 presents the distribution of pressure-group role orientations among lawyers and nonlawyers in the four states. The obvious randomness of the distributions in the table as a whole suggests that being a lawyer or not being a lawyer is evidently not crucial in

---

[16] Robert E. Agger, "Lawyers in Politics," *Temple Law Quarterly*, XXIX (Summer 1956), 436.

[17] *Ibid.*, p. 438.

[18] See Wahlke, *op. cit.*, pp. 323–325. For a fuller discussion, see Wahlke and others, "American State Legislators' Role Orientations toward Pressure Groups," *Journal of Politics*, XXII (May 1960), 213–215.

Table 4.4
Pressure-Group Roles of Lawyers and Nonlawyers

PRESSURE-GROUP ROLE	New Jersey		Ohio		Tennessee		California	
	L	NL	L	NL	L	NL	L	NL
Facilitator	39%	42%	54%	35%	28%	20%	22%	38%
Neutral	34	29	27	38	31	38	33	38
Resister	24	29	15	24	39	38	30	11
Not ascertained	3	0	4	3	2	4	15	13
Total	100%	100%	100%	100%	100%	100%	100%	100%
Number	41	38	59	103	39	81	33	80

the adoption of these orientations. But note differences between the states that are probably symptomatic of different political cultures which, in turn, may affect lawyers' and nonlawyers' pressure-group role conceptions. In the first place, both lawyers and nonlawyers in Tennessee, in almost equal proportions, take the role of resister, and they do so more than legislators anywhere else. The data here seem to support Agger's notion that, to the extent that the political environments of the American South "lack well-organized parties, fewer mediating, negotiating and other intermediary roles are expected since these roles require, by definition, an organizational environment."[19] In fact, as has been noted earlier, though there are fewer groups active in Tennessee than elsewhere, the group struggle there is more bitter, evidently because the facilitating function is not performed.[20]

On the other hand, in the strong two-party systems of New Jersey and Ohio, the facilitator orientation is emphasized and the resister role is minimized by both lawyers and nonlawyers, though the latter seem to be more inclined, if only slightly so, to take the role of resister. In California, finally, where interest groups are abundant,

[19] Agger, op. cit., p. 437.

[20] Wahlke, The Legislative System, pp. 313–323.

greater proportions—and almost equal ones—of both lawyers and nonlawyers appear as neutrals, but lawyers tend to be resisters more and facilitators less than nonlawyers. It is difficult to interpret this outcome, but it may well reflect the fact that at the time of the survey, in 1957, the organizational environment in that traditionally "nonpartisan" state was still weak, making for orientations towards pressure groups that were determined by factors not within the purview of the research.

Some of the *attitudes* expressed by lawyers concerning the activities of pressure groups appear in the following excerpts from interviews in response to the question whether respondents thought the legislature would be better or worse off if lobbies did not try to influence legislation.

Favorable comment:

> If it weren't for lobby groups we'd have worse legislation. It just wouldn't be possible for people to come and express their viewpoints on an individual basis. It is the same situation as with a lawsuit—the individual needs someone to represent his interests. It is through a lobbyist that the individual can get his views expressed. Even if we did prohibit lobbies, we would still listen to the advice and judgment of individuals. In this situation you'd get corporations still hiring a representative to present their viewpoint. This would deny certain groups effective expression of their interests. And labor groups need representatives just as much as corporations.

Neutral comment:

> I used to think it would be better if they weren't around, but we can't eliminate them, we can only regulate them. They are bound to influence some. I have serious doubts that they are as influential as they're thought to be. You do hear some fantastic stories about them. It wouldn't bother me if they were around or not. I haven't heard complaints about them. There is probably some influence. The legislature doesn't need them. A lot of legislators will take advantage of their giving away free drinks, and so on.

Unfavorable comment:

> Without doubt they give you information. But some groups that should be represented have no lobbies. I've a plaintiff's lawyer bill—the insurance people are against it. Lobbyists get what they are after. They would not get what they want if they weren't there. They are around all the time. I'd ban them from the floor even between sessions. Every time I want to do some work, some lobbyist interrupts.

Interest groups are, of course, only one segment of the politician's focus of attention requiring his skills as a negotiator, mediator, or compromiser. He functions in a similar capacity vis-à-vis other clienteles—party organizations, administrative agencies, constituents, and his legislative colleagues. The legislator may take the role of "broker"—a specialist in political integration through negotiation. Some extracts from the interviews may serve to illustrate this role:

> "Politician" has a bad connotation. But it's important to see the other man's point of view. Even if you feel that what you want is the absolute best, give a bit and get the next best thing.

> Generally you should keep an open mind, weigh the testimonies of the committee spokesmen, arguments from the floor, and try to arrive at a decision which will be beneficial to the people of county and state.

> You have the training and background to hear as many sides as you can, and then you have to follow the judgment that this gives you.

> Even though you may express your opinions, you get other opinions too, you learn to keep an open mind; sometimes you see that the others have ideas that are more foresighted than yours and you must forsake your own. It requires a thorough and excellent training in judicial temperament not to jump to conclusions until you've heard the pros and cons of each argument.

Table 4.5 presents the distribution of the broker role orientation among lawyers and nonlawyers in the four states. In New Jersey and California, lawyers take the broker role in slightly greater proportions than do nonlawyers, but the direction is reversed in Ohio.

Table 4.5
Broker Role of Lawyers and Nonlawyers

	New Jersey		Ohio		Tennessee		California	
	L	NL	L	NL	L	NL	L	NL
Per Cent	37	29	46	49	15	15	33	24
Number	41	38	59	103	39	81	33	80

Again, very small, and equal, proportions of lawyers and nonlawyers subscribe to the broker role in Tennessee. This supports the hypothesis that successful performance of the mediating-compromising function is difficult in an environment that is not organizationally structured. In general, the reversal of distributions and the absence of a clear-cut pattern from state to state suggest that, once lawyers and nonlawyers meet in the political arena, differences, if any, do not seem to stem from their divergent occupational backgrounds.

Counselor

Increasingly, as the demands of the business world on the world of law have become more complicated, the modern lawyer has been called upon to give counsel and advice—not only legal advice in anticipation of possible difficulties and their avoidance, but also advice in business matters and other affairs. After the 1880's, writes Hurst,

> The reach and detail of new social regulation, the higher stakes, and the wider range of interests which must be reckoned with in guiding affairs—all these emphasized the lawyer's planning function. Also they put a premium on the hardheaded objectivity of the policy adviser; more and more this was what the client's interests demanded rather than the zealous partisanship of an advocate. Clients were no longer satisfied to put to their lawyers a statement of facts on which to obtain an "opinion." They wanted the lawyer to share the responsibility of deciding what were the determining facts in their situation, to bear part of the weight of fixing policy in the light of the facts so assessed. . . .

. . . The new emphasis was in the lawyer's widening participation in making business policy as a counselor rather than as a co-adventurer.[21]

In the world of politics, the lawyer is similarly called on for policy advice. Indeed, it is in this connection that the traditional law curriculum has come in for criticism. As Myres S. McDougal and Harold D. Lasswell of the Yale Law School wrote twenty years ago, the lawyer

. . . is today, even when not himself a "maker" of policy, the one indispensable adviser of every responsible policy-maker of our society —whether we speak of the head of a government department or agency, of the executive of a corporation or labor union, of the secretary of a trade or other private association, or even of the humble independent enterpriser or professional man. As such an adviser the lawyer, when informing his policy-maker of what he can or cannot legally do, is in an unassailable strategic position to influence, if not create, policy.[22]

Whatever the reason the lawyer's counsel is sought—because of his legal skills proper, his articulateness, or his ability to reconcile conflicting views—he is evidently expected to help in clarifying issues, if not in finding solutions to the perplexities of modern life. If the problems of public policy seem to defy the ingenuity, knowledge, and skills of experts in other professions, there is always, as the economist Jacob Viner once put it rather invidiously, "the lawyer, who is on tap *and* on top, and omnipresent, omniscient, omnipotent, and omnivorous in addition."[23] Not the least concern over the prevalence of lawyers in politics and especially in legislative assemblies stems from apprehensions that the lawyer, his self-

---

[21] Hurst, *op. cit.*, p. 343.

[22] Harold D. Lasswell and Myres S. McDougal, "Legal Education and Public Policy," in Lasswell, *The Analysis of Political Behavior* (New York: Oxford University Press, 1948), p. 27.

[23] Jacob Viner, "The Short View and the Long in Economic Policy," in *The Long View and the Short* (New York: The Free Press of Glencoe, 1958), p. 109.

confidence notwithstanding,[24] is either insufficiently trained to perform the policy-advising or policy-making function, or opposed by
virtue of his training to political change. To what extent the latter
charge is accurate is difficult to tell. Writing over twenty years ago,
Charles S. Hyneman, after surveying what evidence he had, con-
cluded in a wise essay:

> Impelled by this catholicity of self-interest and fortified by num-
> bers, the lawyer group in the legislature stands as a potential ob-
> struction to every statutory innovation. The force of this resistance
> has never been objectively measured; my own observations suggest
> that the literature greatly overstates its importance.[25]

What evidence is there for the lawyer's stance as a legislative
policy-maker compared with the nonlawyer? Among legislative
roles that of "inventor" seems to be directly relevant.[26] Of course,
under modern conditions the formulation of public policy has increasingly become the function of the executive branch, or it is the
product of suggestions and pressures from the private sector of society. Yet, whatever the realities of the situation, the contemporary
legislator still seems to see himself as a policy-maker.

Table 4.6 presents lawyers' and nonlawyers' inventor role orientations. As the table shows, lawyers differ very little from nonlawyers
in articulating this role. In New Jersey and Ohio the lawyers, and
in Tennessee the nonlawyers, are only slightly more inclined to
mention the inventor role.

---

[24] See Riesman, "Problems of Method in the Social Sciences," in *op. cit.*, p.
435: "How often have I sat with a group of lawyers and heard one of them say,
'Of course, I know nothing about it, but. . . .' The lawyer's feeling that he could
master anything in a pre-trial two weeks, that there is no expertise but his own,
is often arrogant and Philistine, and I used frequently to have to argue with my
brethren of the bar that neither economics nor anthropology could be so easily
encompassed."

[25] Charles S. Hyneman, "Who Makes Our Laws?" in John C. Wahlke and
Heinz Eulau (eds.), *Legislative Behavior* (New York: The Free Press of Glencoe,
1959), p. 264.

[26] For an elaboration of this role orientation, see Wahlke, *op. cit.*, pp. 248
and 254–256.

Table 4.6
Inventor Role of Lawyers and Nonlawyers

	New Jersey		Ohio		Tennessee		California	
	L	NL	L	NL	L	NL	L	NL
Per Cent	51	47	37	30	28	31	36	34
Number	41	38	59	103	39	81	33	80

Lawyers evidently are not more or less policy-oriented than non-lawyers. This too suggests that the political arena eliminates differences that one might expect if lawyers played functional roles in the private sphere that differ from political roles in the public sphere. The inventor role as such does not, of course, tell us whether the legislator is conservative or liberal. But the distributions do suggest that lawyers are at least as much concerned with policy, whatever its direction, as are other politicians.

Contact Man

A final role of the lawyer—perhaps the most recent in origin of all—which stems from his relationship with clients, is that of "contact man," as Harold L. Wilensky termed it in his discussion of lawyers in labor unions:

> . . . The Contact Man "arrives" more through his skills in private consultation, negotiation, and mediation and his intimate knowledge of the workings of his union and of American society, than through his knowledge of contracts, constitutions, statutes, and deeds, or his skill in the courtroom. "The best thing you can have" to make out as a labor lawyer, says one Contact Man, "is a general social science background. Most of what we do isn't connected with the law anyway. . . . A lot of it is public relations. You act as a go-between."[27]

The lawyer's wide contacts enable him to intervene wherever his services are needed, and they give him access to information—and

---

[27] Harold L. Wilensky, *Intellectuals in Labor Unions* (New York: The Free Press of Glencoe, 1956), pp. 62–63.

with information, presumably, influence—that is less readily available to members of most professions. As Ferdinand Lundberg wrote more than twenty years ago, the lawyer

> . . . either knows all there is to know about judges, public officials, business leaders, bankers, professional politicians, labor leaders, newspaper publishers, leading clergymen, and the like, or through that informal clearing house of esoteric information, the bar association, can find out from colleagues. The lawyer is a vast reservoir of actual or potential information about the social and political topography. . . .[28]

Robert Agger speaks of the lawyer's "linking function" in the local community between decision-makers in different areas of policy-making, which he ascribes to the lawyer's close connection with other lawyers, judges, government officials, and clients.[29] In their insightful study of a small, rural New York community, the sociologists Arthur J. Vidich and Joseph Bensman explicitly note the functional equivalence of the lawyer's contact role on the personal level and the political party's role on the institutional level:

> Power in local political affairs, then, tends to be based on accessibility to sources of decision in larger institutions. Frequently this accessibility consists merely of the knowledge of the source, or it may mean a personal contact, or an ability to correspond to get necessary information. Under these circumstances, power in the political arena is delegated to those with contacts in and knowledge of the outer world and to those who are experts in formal communication with impersonal bureaucratic offices. These are, on the individual level, the lawyer and, on the institutional level, the political party. The lawyer gains his paramountcy through technical knowledge and personalized non-party contacts up the political hierarchy with other lawyers. He is the mediator between the local party and the party hierarchy, and transforms his personalized contacts into political indispensability in

---

[28] Ferdinand Lundberg, "The Profession of the Law," *Harper's*, CLVIII (September 1958), 10.

[29] Agger, *op. cit.*, p. 442.

the local community. His access to outside sources of power determines his power and predominance in the local community.[30]

What is said of the lawyer as "contact man" may also be said of the politician. He, too, is a contact man; multiple public and private connections stem from his interstitial position in the social and political structure. What is sometimes called the "errand-boy" function—including communicative activities such as helping people with their problems, contacting administrative agencies for constituents, finding jobs for them, making speeches before clubs, writing newspaper columns, and so on—has long been recognized as an important component of the legislator's total role.[31] The following extracts from interviews will convey some of the conceptions that go into this interpretation of the legislator's role:

> [The job is] helping individual citizens with problems, on the federal level such as with immigration problems, on the state level such as with licensing of engineers, for instance; explaining to someone why he has been rejected and what he can do about it; also other sundry claims.

> Also, there is a certain service to be rendered, as an intermediary between state offices and agencies and his constituents. The legislator acts as a source of information; and he should keep constituents informed on matters affecting them.

> Keep up with correspondence, keep them informed on legislation I'm interested in. I've done this, on bills I've authored and co-authored. If you mentioned an issue in the campaign, keep them informed on it. Take care of little problems for constituents, with state departments check on complications and problems. An example: A fellow wanted to find out why he had to work two years after he was seventy to qualify for a pension—the county engineer had failed to deduct his share for retirement.

---

[30] Arthur J. Vidich and Joseph Bensman, *Small Town in Mass Society* (Garden City, N.Y.: Doubleday & Company, Anchor Books, 1960), p. 102. For a description of the community's legal counsel and his contacts, see *ibid.*, pp. 222–223.

[31] For a discussion of the legislator's communication and service functions, see Wahlke, *op. cit.*, pp. 304–308.

A lot of people from your county want something taken care of; you should be available to guide them around public bodies. I'm not sure this is part of the primary job, but it's a concept of local people.

As all these quotations suggest, the legislator as "errand-boy" sees himself, or is seen, as the chief link between his district and the state. In his decision-making behavior, also, he has a choice of orienting himself toward both district and state as main foci of attention (or, of course, toward his district alone or the state alone).[32] The district-state orientation particularly serves the important function of integrating the interests of the district and those of the state in the legislative consensus.

If the lawyer were to be more a contact man than his nonlawyer colleague as a result of his connections, he might be expected to take the double-barreled "district-state" role more than the nonlawyer. The data presented in Table 4.7 do not support this hy-

Table 4.7

Areal Roles of Lawyers and Nonlawyers

	New Jersey		Ohio		Tennessee		California	
AREAL ROLE	L	NL	L	NL	L	NL	L	NL
District-State	37%	18%	20%	28%	8%	9%	15%	14%
District	20	34	24	31	18	22	24	40
State	10	18	19	15	5	11	12	20
Not ascertained	33	30	37	26	69	58	49	26
Total	100%	100%	100%	100%	100%	100%	100%	100%
Number	41	38	59	103	39	81	33	80

pothesis. Only in New Jersey do lawyer-legislators tend to take this hyphenated role in greater proportions than do nonlawyers. In Ohio the direction is reversed; and in Tennessee and California there is hardly any difference at all. On the other hand, it is significant that

---

[32] For a fuller description of these role orientations, see *ibid.*, pp. 288–291.

in all four states nonlawyers take the solo district role consistently in greater proportions than do lawyers, suggesting that the lawyer's focus of attention, when polarized, is less parochial and more cosmopolitan than that of the nonlawyer, as one might well expect in view of the lawyer's greater exposure to educational opportunities. It should be pointed out, however, that the data presented in Table 4.7 are probably highly unstable because of the great number of respondents; especially in Tennessee and California, whose areal role orientations could not be ascertained. The following replies from interviews illustrate how lawyer-legislators articulate the dual "contact role" of the "district-state-oriented" politician:

> Each man here has a dual obligation. He must keep in mind the needs of his constituents and how every bill would affect them, but he must also look at the state as a whole and try to determine what is beneficial for the whole area.

> A legislator is sent from his district to represent; however, he should be able to consider problems as they affect the state as a whole. He can become so wrapped up in his own problems that he is not serving effectively.

> It is also necessary to keep in mind the problems and needs of your local community. You should see that their cause and interests are given proper consideration, while at the same time taking into consideration the balancing of equities. You must not give undue consideration to one group over that of another.

A DIVERGENT ROLE: THE LAWYER AS AN EXPERT

Even though lawyer- and nonlawyer-legislators differ little from one another in most of the roles they assume as legislators, lawyers may yet stand out in some respects, especially in areas related directly to the more narrowly defined "legal" skills they acquire as a result of their specialized education or practice. Certainly, the lawyer does things that the politician does not do—he drafts documents, untangles complicated raw facts, weighs these facts in counseling clients, and chooses the legal tools with which to pursue a case. Indeed, the modern lawyer is a "master of fact." The late Justice Louis Brandeis articulated this role in a memorandum on "What the practice of the law includes," setting down certain axioms: "Know thoroughly each fact. Don't believe client witness. Examine documents. Reason; use imagination. Know bookkeeping—the universal language of business: know persons. Far more likely to impress clients by knowledge of facts than by knowledge of law. . . . Know not only specific case, but whole subject. Can't otherwise know these facts. Know not only those facts which bear on direct controversy, but know all the facts and law that surround."[33]

In the modern legislature, specialized knowledge is as much the politician's staple as is an understanding of public policies. One of the surprising findings of the larger project was that, counter to prevailing notions about the politician's being a jack-of-all-trades, legislative behavior seems to be characterized by a considerable degree of specialization and expertise.[34] The lawyer's specialty, even after he has become a member of a legislature, is "the law." In that area, at least, his expertise should distinguish him from the nonlawyer. Beyond that, as he masters a professional specialization in fact, he might be expected to be more reluctant than the nonlawyer to see himself as an "expert" in several areas of specialization. David Gold has reported that

> In looking for evidence of role differences in data provided by the various state registers, a most obvious source is the make-up of the legislative committees. It may appear surprising at first consideration that, with the exception of the judiciary committees of one sort or another, lawyers show no special concentration on any particular committees. However, it seems significant that lawyers have proportionate representation on committees across-the-board regardless of the specialized nature of any given sub-committee. For example, in two Midwestern states lawyers are only slightly underrepresented on

---

[33] Quoted by Alpheus Thomas Mason, *Brandeis, A Free Man's Life* (New York: The Viking Press, 1946), p. 69.

[34] See Wahlke, *op. cit.*, "Subject Matter Experts," Chapter 9, pp. 193–215.

committees dealing particularly with farm problems. In terms of politics, the lawyer appears to be considered a jack-of-all-trades; not so the farmer, he does not serve on the judiciary committee.[35]

Table 4.8 presents some evidence from this study. Although the differences are small, in all states fewer of the lawyers than of the nonlawyers designated themselves as "expert" in three or more areas of specialization. Moreover, except in Tennessee, lawyers were more inclined than nonlawyers to lay no claim to expertise at all or to refer to themselves as "generalists." It would seem that lawyers are more

Table 4.8

Number of Areas of Expertise

NUMBER OF AREAS OF EXPERTISE	New Jersey		Ohio		Tennessee		California	
	L	NL	L	NL	L	NL	L	NL
Three or more	24%	31%	22%	27%	13%	14%	37%	41%
One or two	49	63	60	57	61	57	50	56
None	12	3	17	12	21	26	9	3
"Generalist"	15	3	0	4	3	4	3	1
Total	100%	100%	100%	100%	100%	100%	100%	100%
Number	41	38	59	103	39	81	33	80

sensitive than nonlawyers to the meaning of "expertise." The true expert is expert in only one field and, by definition, cannot be expert in many. Recognizing this, the lawyer in politics seems to be modest in claiming expertise and in seeing himself as a jack-of-all-trades.

In what areas do lawyer-legislators designate themselves as experts? Table 4.9 presents the distributions of self-designations. As the italicized figures in the table show, more expert self-designations with regard to specific fields were made by lawyers in all four states in only two fields—law and its various aspects, and legislative procedure. In three states lawyer nominations exceeded nonlawyer

---

[35] David Gold, "Lawyers in Politics," *Pacific Sociological Review*, IV (Fall 1961), 86.

Table 4.9

Self-Designations as "Experts"*

AREAS OF EXPERTISE	New Jersey		Ohio		Tennessee		California	
	L	NL	L	NL	L	NL	L	NL
Law (code revision, enforcement, civil rights, criminal)	22%	5%	32%	1%	47%	4%	20%	3%
Legislative procedure (drafting)	2	0	10	**	2	0	5	**
Local government	18	4	5	5	5	4	8	5
Insurance	3	1	1	2	2	5	5	2
Labor relations	2	10	8	6	4	4	5	2
Military veterans	6	4	0	1	2	0	0	3
Education	12	10	11	17	9	11	5	11
Conservation	8	9	1	5	0	3	15	12
Public finance	3	4	5	15	7	5	3	7
State government	5	3	1	4	0	1	6	6
Agriculture	5	3	0	10	5	13	3	10
Welfare	0	12	7	7	5	5	0	6
Transportation	5	5	7	9	2	9	6	6
Health	3	8	2	2	0	13	2	4
Other (less than 5% in any area)	6	22	10	14	10	23	17	22
Total	100%	100%	100%	100%	100%	100%	100%	100%
Number	69	76	84	169	56	101	67	183

* Because respondents could name themselves as "expert" in more than one field and because our interest here is in the proportions of nominations, the percentages are based on the total number of self-designations rather than on the number of individuals making them. The italicized figures indicate the fields in any state where lawyers' self-designations exceed those of nonlawyers.

** Less than one per cent.

designations in the field of local government. In two states the same was true of insurance, labor, and military or veterans' affairs; it was true with education, conservation, public finance, state government, and agriculture in only one state. That lawyers should be so predominant in the legal field is, of course, not surprising. Otherwise, their self-designations are scattered. Taking ten per cent of nominations as the dividing line, the table shows that lawyers named themselves quite often also as experts in a number of other fields. In general, it seems that, though he may be a "master of many facts," the lawyer is still most comfortable in his own field as it has traditionally been defined. The following quotations from the interviews, in response to the question how the job of legislator might be described, convey the lawyer's legal-technical orientation:

> The most important thing, which isn't done enough, is to watch the type of bills that pass and to watch the language of the bills. A legislator should be very sure that the language of the bill actually conveys the intent of the bill.

> The most essential is being as familiar as possible with the legislation proposed and its effects. He should do detailed work in preparing legislation so it is in good form when it is introduced. We should all have a great capacity for work along legal lines.

> To make sure that bills presented to the legislature do not conflict with the code. Bills should be in proper form so that they carry out their purpose.

The lawyer's commitment to his professional background as he relates himself to his work as legislator also appears from the "reasons" given by the respondents for their expertise. As Table 4.10 shows, in every one of the four states lawyers mentioned their occupational or associational background as a reason in greater proportion than did nonlawyers, though in California, particularly, the difference is very small. On the other hand, nonlawyers tended more than lawyers to give reasons referring to personal interest or involvement—a category that refers either to some past experience with the field or to some general expression that the respondent con-

Table 4.10

Reasons for Expertise*

REASONS FOR EXPERTISE	New Jersey		Ohio		Tennessee		California	
	L	NL	L	NL	L	NL	L	NL
Occupational experience	37%	24%	48%	38%	65%	50%	26%	24%
Legislative assignment (committee)	8	14	29	24	8	13	19	18
Political experience	15	15	0	2	0	1	8	7
Problems important to district experience	19	5	2	5	5	5	18	16
Other personal experience or involvement	21	42	21	31	22	31	29	35
Total	100%	100%	100%	100%	100%	100%	100%	100%
Number	48	59	62	126	40	84	62	155

* Since respondents could name more than one field and different reasons for expertise in the same field, or in different fields, percentages are based on the total number of responses, 636, given by 395 respondents.

---

siders the field important. With regard to other reasons, the responses are quite random. In other words, his occupation does seem to make a difference in the way in which the lawyer approaches the more technical aspects of lawmaking. Some comments from the interviews, again, will serve to illustrate lawyers' orientations in this respect:

> Well, I'm a lawyer and members started coming to me to read their bills and see if they were all right constitutionally. Pretty soon I got a reputation for having experience in these matters and everyone started coming to me. I have been a lawyer for twenty-eight years, I've had many years of experience.

I practice law in those fields and I represent the labor unions in my law business.

I'm an attorney and interested in being a judge. After you've been here a while, you get to know how to draft bills.

I spent five years preparing to be an attorney-at-law, and as a lawyer I represent three transportation companies.

Most important is my contribution as a lawyer of twenty years' experience in municipal work and educational work. . . . Application of this background toward legislation.

A nonlawyer's appreciation of the lawyer was expressed in this comment:

When you go to a man and ask his counsel, you may disagree with his philosophy, but he gives you a true answer as he sees it. . . . This is especially true of lawyers. Others of us have to consult them frequently and they always tell us the truth.

THE LAWYER AS LEGISLATIVE LEADER

A few lawyers in all four states named themselves as experts in legislative procedure, which includes knowledge and skill in parliamentary law. It is plausible to assume that these skills place the lawyer in a favorable position to be recruited into legislative leadership offices or to be appointed to committees especially concerned with the legislature's work flow, such as committees on rules, calendar, or reference. "Lawyers' importance in both national and state legislatures," Hurst has noted, "was heightened by the importance of the committee assignments and the committee chairmanships which they usually held."[36] This, it seems, was the case especially after 1850: Lawyers "generally controlled or were especially prominent in rules or steering committees, directing the general procedure and order

---

[36] Hurst, *op. cit.*, p. 47.

of business. . . . This pattern meant that lawyer members had great power in the management of legislative programs."[37]

Table 4.11 compares the proportions of lawyers serving as officers, committee chairmen, or members of important procedural committees in the four states with the proportions of lawyers in the legislatures as wholes. The data confirm what one might expect. In New Jersey, the only state where lawyers outnumber the nonlawyers, two-thirds of the officer positions and more than half of the procedural committees are manned by lawyers, though the proportion of lawyers in committee chairmanships falls below the total proportion of lawyers in the legislature. In Ohio and Tennessee, lawyers

Table 4.11
Lawyers in Important Legislative Posts

	% total lawyers in legislature	% lawyers of officers	% lawyers of chairmen	% lawyers of procedural committee members
New Jersey	52 (N=79)	67 (N=9)	42 (N=24)	54 (N=24)
Ohio	36 (N=173)	67 (N=6)	40 (N=45)	46 (N=37)
Tennessee	30 (N=132)	57 (N=7)	38 (N=29)	43 (N=53)
California	30 (N=120)	29 (N=7)	23 (N=44)	25 (N=12)

appear as officers, chairmen, or procedural committee members in greater proportions than the total proportion of their profession in these legislatures would lead one to expect. In California, finally, lawyers in all these positions are proportionately fewer than their proportion in the legislature as a whole would lead one to anticipate. But this is not especially surprising. It must be recalled that in California lawyers as a group had considerably less legislative experience

---

[37] *Ibid.*, pp. 352–353. Hurst *speculates* that, "on the other hand, it probably meant a lessened influence on policy in important areas dominated by modern interest groups and voting blocs (such as those concerning agriculture or trade practices), and in important fields of the service activity of modern government (as in education)." There is, as far as we know, no evidence for or against this statement.

than nonlawyers, their median length of service being only 2.8 years as against 6.8 years for the nonlawyers. Seniority, it seems, is a necessary requisite, in California at least, for appointment to critical legislative jobs or committees.[38]

In his occupancy of important positions in the legislature, the lawyer's professional background and role appear to distinguish him, though not in a consistent way, from members of other occupations. Lawyers, it seems, are recognized as being particularly well fitted to fill such positions and to assume the leadership roles that must be taken in any such institutionalized group as a legislature.

On the other hand, the political culture of the legislature, common to both lawyer and nonlawyer members, provides for those norms of behavior that are expected to guide every politician's conduct, regardless what his special private roles or public roles may be. The norms of political conduct, or "rules of the game," represent that "working consensus" without which no human group can survive as a group. Many of the rules circumscribing legislative behavior are, of course, formal or "standing" regulations. But many are informal understandings, transmitted by word or precept from oldtimers to newcomers within any particular institutional arena. More than forty such rules were identified in the four states studied, and they could be classified into five functional categories—functional, that is, to the operation of the legislature as a human group quite independent of the particular incumbents of legislative positions at any particular time: (1) rules primarily promoting group cohesion and solidarity; (2) rules primarily making for predictability of behavior; (3) rules primarily channeling and restraining conflict; (4) rules primarily expediting the legislative business; and (5) rules primarily serving to give tactical advantages to individual members.

---

[38] But what of Ohio, where nonlawyers, as in California, had longer service than lawyers? The answer is simple: In Ohio, seniority was deliberately eschewed as a criterion for appointment to positions of leadership. As the Ohio House President *pro tem.* (assistant majority leader) told the interviewer: "To get the most efficient work done, we like to appoint young, well-educated lawyers to these jobs."

If the notion that these rules constitute the legislature's working consensus is correct, it may be expected that there will be no significant differences between incumbent lawyer- and nonlawyer-legislators' responses concerning the rules of the game, for both groups should be equally affected by the do's and don't's of the informal normative system that presumably regulates at least some aspects of their conduct as legislators. Two measures will be used to examine the working consensus—an index of "extent of sensitivity" to the rules of the game, based on the number of rules that are named, and an index of "diversity of sensitivity," based on the number of types of rules that are mentioned in the interviews.

Table 4.12
Lawyers' and Nonlawyers' Sensitivity to the Rules of the Game

	New Jersey		Ohio		Tennessee		California	
	L	NL	L	NL	L	NL	L	NL
Mean extent of sensitivity to rules of the game	3.8	3.7	3.6	3.5	4.1	3.7	4.4	4.0
Mean diversity of sensitivity to the rules of the game	2.7	2.5	2.4	2.4	2.7	2.6	2.5	2.4

Table 4.12 presents the mean number of rules and types of rules for lawyers and nonlawyers in the four state legislatures. For all practical purposes, there are no differences in extent and diversity of sensitivity to the rules of the game. Even though nothing can be said here on the specific rules mentioned by lawyers and nonlawyers, two measures at least indicate that in all four legislatures there is a general consensus that such rules exist and that, by implication, legislators are bound to live by them.

CONCLUSION

Comparison of lawyers and nonlawyers in regard to the roles they take as legislators indicates both similarities and some differences between the professions. No differences, or only random distributions, are found in regard to political roles that may be considered functional equivalents of certain legal roles. But, in regard to roles that are highly differentiated in terms of legislators' prepolitical occupational skills and experiences, such as the expert or leader roles, lawyers differ from nonlawyers. In these roles the lawyer dominates not as a politician but in his identity as a lawyer. Some tentative theoretical explorations and explanations of these results are presented in the next chapter.

Chapter 5

THE CONVERGENCE OF PROFESSIONS

Preoccupation with real or alleged dysfunctional consequences of the lawyer's ubiquity in politics has had the effect of orienting research toward analysis of differences rather than of similarities in the behavior of the politician who is a lawyer and the politician who is not. Because the lawyer is more visible in politics than any other private-occupational type, with the possible exception of the farmer, it is easy enough to assume not only that he is different, but that whatever differentiates him from the nonlawyer pervades his conduct in public life and has identifiable effects on the functioning of a political system. "My notion is," writes the sociologist David Gold,

> that by virtue of training, experience, and perhaps a prior process of selectivity, the lawyer is apt to behave differently *in the political arena* than the nonlawyer.[1]

It is, of course, a very conventional sociological assumption—for which there is a good deal of evidence—that a man's total perspective is crucially conditioned by his position in the social structure and notably by the structure of occupations. But many of the data presented in the preceding chapters suggest that the standard sociological formula may have to be modified. Lawyer-politicians do not differ much from politicians who are not lawyers. Now, most

---

[1] David Gold, "Lawyers in Politics: An Empirical Exploration of Biographical Data on State Legislators," *The Pacific Sociological Review*, IV (Fall 1961), 84.

studies of lawyers in politics, discovering only slight differences between lawyers and others, or no differences at all, usually conclude
on a somewhat disappointed note. Paradoxically, the conclusion of
such a study may sound triumphant: Does not the absence of significant differences between lawyers and nonlawyers in politics
prove that a man's occupation has little to do with his public
decision-making behavior? Does it not prove that he can transcend
whatever narrow viewpoints may be associated with his occupation
and rise to the responsibility of a public career by giving disinterested service—disinterested, that is, in terms of his occupational
background and predispositions?

But the function of occupation in politics need not be denied
simply because it cannot be directly confirmed by comparing lawyers with nonlawyers and noting the absence of differences between
them. In fact, the affinity of law and politics as vocations suggests
the need for a theoretical formulation of the problem which, on the
one hand, does not reject the general hypothesis that a man's occupation is critical in his political behavior but which, on the other hand,
allows for treating the lawyer's role in politics as a special case.

The intellectual problem involved in formulating an empirically
viable conception of the lawyer's role in politics stems from the
notion, well articulated by Max Weber, that the lawyer is proto-
typical of the modern professional politician.[2] But this cannot mean
that nonlawyers in politics are, as if by automatic exclusion, less able
politicians. The conventional search for differences between lawyers
and nonlawyers in politics ignores what we think is an assumption
that must necessarily be made about the political system in which
both are involved—namely, that the polity constitutes an autonomous
system of role relationships with a culture of its own that makes for
attitudes, values, and styles of behavior that are characteristic of the
political as contrasted with any other type of social system. Both
lawyers and nonlawyers are "socialized" into this political culture,
which is sufficiently pervasive to have an impact on political practitioners regardless what their private occupations are or have been.

---

[2] See Reinhard Bendix, *Max Weber: An Intellectual Portrait* (Garden City,
N.Y.: Doubleday & Company, 1960), p. 436.

However, it does not suffice to argue that the roles imposed on the participants in a political system are so penetrating that all other influences are nullified. This would be equivalent to arguing that individual determinants of political behavior are of no theoretical interest or practical importance because the present situation in which an individual finds himself is inevitably the controlling circumstance. Aside from the drastic nature of such a proposition, its disregard of the existence of *some kind* of intimate relationship between law and politics is precisely what leads us to reject it. In effect, it sidesteps the problem of explanation that the data call for.

In particular, this comparison of lawyers and nonlawyers revealed two empirical phenomena that must be accommodated in a theoretical formulation that can help in accounting for both. On the one hand, the review of their political backgrounds and careers, reported in Chapter 3, indicated that lawyers in politics may well be politicians first, chronologically speaking, whose political orientation precedes their choice of law as a private pursuit and who enter the profession of law in order to promote better their political aspirations. In other words, what Woodrow Wilson said of himself—that he "chose" politics as his profession, but that he "entered" the law as a profession because he thought that entering the one would lead to the other—may well be true of the lawyer-politician generally. There are likely to be exceptions to the rule, of course. But entering the profession of law in order to pursue a career in politics would seem to make sense only, given the far-reaching character of the career choice, if the two professions are somehow accounted for in a single system of explanation.

On the other hand, juxtaposition of some of the roles taken by lawyer- and nonlawyer-legislators in their public clientele relationships, such as those of trustee, tribune, facilitator, broker, inventor, and so on, and the roles taken by lawyers in their private client relationships, such as those of fiduciary, advocate, attorney, counselor, or contact man, suggested their functional equivalence. This functional equivalence, it would seem, goes a long way in accounting for the fact that lawyers and nonlawyers do not differ as they assume legislative roles in terms of which they relate themselves to their legislative tasks, or that they seem to take legislative roles in an arbitrary manner. But functional equivalence is an empirical phenomenon that itself requires theoretical explication.

In order to come to theoretical grips with the problem, consider the notion of "professional convergence." This, it will appear, is a strictly theoretical construct that must not be confused with the affinity or compatibility of law and politics as professions in empirical reality. For it is this affinity that the concept of professional convergence is supposed to explain. Rather, the notion of convergence posits the isomorphism of the two professions: Although they are distinct and structurally independent of each other as professions, law and politics come to exhibit similar forms—a convergence which, it is postulated, would have occurred even if law and politics did not in reality intersect with one another as professions.

For the purpose of explicating the concept of professional convergence, we assume that, were convergence *not* to occur, relevant professional characteristics would be distributed at random among *all* the various professions. To put this positively, professional convergence is present if two professions have common characteristics that are especially relevant to the performance of professional functions, while a third, fourth, or fifth profession does not share these attributes. In the case of law and politics, for instance, there are functionally equivalent roles in terms of which the professions can be analyzed. One task of research, then, is to discover the conditions under which two professions are likely to be convergent.

"Convergence" is a developmental concept. It refers to a tendency or trend of two phenomena to develop similar forms. When speaking of "professional convergence," then, as in the case of law and politics as vocations, we mean that these professions will come to exhibit similar forms as a result of developmental tendencies in response to the society's needs and to the demands that are made by the society on both professions.

It is not the intention of this book to construct a theory of professional convergence, but rather to clarify the concept in terms of some theoretical assumptions that must be made if the concept is to serve the heuristic objective for which it is being formulated. The central assumption is that law and politics, though of different ancestry *as professions*, are isomorphic—that is, similar in structure because of convergent development; and that, because convergence is conceived as a continuous process, the similarity will "grow" as time goes on. Although the terms used here are theoretical, not empirical, convergence can be demonstrated. But at the same time it should be emphasized that an isomorphism is never complete. In other words, it does not cover the whole range of empirically observable phenomena. On the other hand, it is meant to be a "true representation" of the phenomena to be observed. For instance, a map is not a complete representation of the terrain, but a good map is a true representation: It permits the reader to locate himself accurately in the terrain. Because a theoretical construct is necessarily abstract, it refers only to selected aspects of the phenomena that may be observed, and it omits other aspects. A map symbolizes the relations between aspects of the terrain, but it is not in one-to-one correspondence with the terrain. Indeed, if a map (or model) were a "replica" of empirical reality, no new knowledge, even of a descriptive kind, would be forthcoming—for all that might be observed would have been observed already.[3]

The assumption of convergence, then, is especially applicable in comparing two phenomena that have properties and relations between these properties that are similar (or better, that are postulated to be similar). But this does not mean that the two phenomena are identical. If they were identical, there could be no discussion of isomorphism. Applied to the present concern, then, law and politics are descriptively distinct. They are not considered, for theoretical purposes, to act directly upon one another. Although law and politics as professions may be structurally isomorphic, no connection between them need be assumed. Because of convergence, however,

---

[3] May Brodbeck, "Models, Meaning, and Theories," in Llewellyn Gross (ed.), *Symposium on Sociological Theory* (Evanston, Ill.: Row, Peterson & Company, 1959), p. 374.

both exhibit the same set of "logical" relations or "common" properties, so that a single type of conceptualization will fit both.

Although two phenomena may perform similar functions, they need not be structurally isomorphic. This fact is often observed in studies of political functions that are performed by structurally quite different organizations. Political parties in multiparty systems, for instance, perform many of the functions that, in a two-party system, are performed by interest groups, and vice versa. Thus, the argument presented here does not rest on the premise that, as a matter of undemonstrable assumption, there *must* be some structural similarities between parties when similar functions are carried out by different structures. From the theoretical point of view, such a relationship must be demonstrated empirically and spelled out in precise detail to be admissible as an explanation.

That professional convergence of law and politics is evident, then, does not mean that law and politics have merged or will merge into a single profession, or that one profession will be absorbed by the other. Nor does it mean that one profession is identical with the other in internal structure, in external relations, or in the functions it performs both internally and externally. Law and politics are quite distinct, each having its own unique ways of socializing an individual into the profession, recruiting him to a particular post and assigning him particular tasks, transmitting professional knowledge and lore, forming and enforcing its norms of proper conduct. The two are distinct with regard to the institutional settings in which each performs its functions, and these functions remain in many respects quite different. This discussion merely postulates that the two professions converge in an isomorphic sense.

To avoid misunderstanding, the argument can be restated briefly. A similarity (not identity) between law and politics as professions can be shown to exist empirically; this similarity can be specified precisely in theoretical terms; and accurate operations can be performed that will allow measurement of the similarity. This is, of course, a very strong set of assumptions. But in the cases where the tasks that the three assumptions specify can be accomplished, it can be said that an isomorphism between law and politics exists. Remember that we have not as yet carried out these tasks in regard to the professions of law and politics, but only made the theoretical problem more precise. It remains to delineate the relationship of the structural isomorphism of the two professions to the developmental concept of professional convergence.

The assumption here is that structural isomorphism is a product of a similar development of the two professions. That is to say, similar development over time has resulted in acquisition of similar properties and similar relationships between properties by the professions of law and politics. This development can be viewed as a process of which the beginning point may not be clear but for which the end point may be precisely stated. The end point is that point at which an isomorphism exists between two professions, in the strong sense that professional membership no longer differentiates any relevant aspect of behavior. This is the point, in the present case of law and politics, where all lawyers (and not just lawyer-politicians) behave precisely as politicians who are not lawyers behave, and the converse.

The fact that the beginning of the development of convergence cannot be clearly specified is of little theoretical importance. It can be assumed that the initial point is one at which law and politics are not closely related and at which the behavior of lawyers in politics clearly differentiates them from other politicians as much as from other persons with differing occupations or social roles.

The theoretical argument may now be restated. If two professions exhibit similar developments with respect to specified properties characteristic of these professions, they are in the process of converging. If the two professions are in the process of converging, then they will show a structural isomorphism that is dependent, first, on the similarity of the development of the properties deemed relevant and, second, on the opportunity for such development (i.e., "time"). If two professions are highly convergent, they will exhibit an isomorphism with properties approximating those of the theoretical end point of the convergence process—that is, professional membership will not differentiate behavior. In the empirical context of this study, if lawyers and politicians belong to converging professions, then law and politics as professions are isomorphic. If law and politics are isomorphs, *and* if this isomorphism approximates the end point of the theoretical convergence process, then it may be expected that lawyers will not differ in their political behavior from other politicians. And this seems to be true.

It is well to keep in mind that convergence may not lead to similarity in all respects. There remain matters, for instance, in which the functions of lawyer as lawyer and of politician as politician do not converge, and in which corresponding roles in fact diverge. This, as has been noted in Chapter 4, seems to be the case with roles that require specialized expertise and skill in parliamentary leadership. The lawyer who becomes active as a politician, regardless whether his primary commitment is to law or to politics, still remains a lawyer, so that, when his legislative activity involves specialized problems directly relevant to his private occupation, especially legal or constitutional matters, he differs from the non-lawyer in the roles he takes. He is more likely to name fewer areas of "expertise," and, among those he names, "law" predominates. Moreover, in giving reasons for his expertise, in law or in other fields, the lawyer is more likely than the nonlawyer to refer to his private-professional background and experience. Similarly, as an expert in parliamentary law and procedure, the lawyer as lawyer seems to have an advantage over the nonlawyer-politician in that he is more "available" for roles of legislative leadership. In these two empirical aspects, then, the professions of law and politics seem to be more divergent than convergent, for the moment at least.

One final point must be emphasized before we attempt to suggest some content for the convenient assumptions that have so far been made. The properties and relationships between properties that remain to be specified are properties of the professions as aggregates, independent of the characteristics of any particular individual member of the profession. In other words, any particular person may not in fact participate in the relationships that are asserted to be typical of his profession. For example, it will be suggested that an ethics of service is characteristic of both law and politics as professions. But this does not imply that any particular lawyer or politician accepts such an ethics as his own. Over-all, of course, the assertions must be true for a preponderance of those members of the professions that are included in any empirical study.

CONDITIONS OF CONVERGENCE

In turning to the problem of specifying those properties and relationships that have undergone the process of convergence and now constitute for law and politics elements of a structural isomorphism between the two professions, we shall initially suggest two conditions for convergence in this particular case. First, both law and politics as professions tend to be integrated into the structure of political authority; and, second, both exhibit similar tendencies, within their distinct areas of authority and competence, to perform functions either political in nature or depending on the governmental and political system. These conditions of the political system tend to make for the convergence of the two professions by facilitating the lawyer's adaptability to the political sphere, and also, as later sections will suggest, the politician's preference for law as a private occupation.

That the politician is integrated into the structure of the political system may seem self-evident today, but it is well to recall that he has not always been an "insider." His integration has been a relatively slow, secular process. This is not the place to recapitulate the growth of representative institutions in the West, but the broad outline may be suggested. The medieval "representative," whether he was found in the English Parliament, the Spanish Cortez, or any other "representative" body, was not regarded as an official of the government. He stood in well-defined relations of more or less dependence to political authority, but he was not himself a direct participant in that authority. His integration into the political system was not direct but was mediated by his membership in the subsidiary estates or corporations whose representative he was vis-à-vis political authority. Only in the course of centuries, as representative assemblies gradually replaced the Crown and its bureaucracy as effective centers of power, did the politician become directly responsible for public policy-making—that is, integrated into the structure of political authority. But no more need be said about this here, since the integration of the elective public official in the structure of political authority is well beyond doubt in democratic societies.

The lawyer's relation to political authority is somewhat more complex. As Talcott Parsons has pointed out, the legal profession "is in a curiously ambiguous position of dependence and independence with reference to the state. The laws for which it is responsible are official enactments of the state. . . . The member of the bar is formally an 'officer of the court,' and for example, disbarment is an act of the political authority." At the same time, Parsons continues, "and at least equally important, the profession is independent of political authority. Even judges, though public officials, are treated as in a special class with special immunities."[4]

The lawyer's ascendancy in politics coincided, in the eighteenth century and again in the nineteenth, with periods of commercial and economic growth—that is, periods of increasing division of labor. While, as a result of this division, both lawyers and politicians came to assume specialized roles, they are in a particularly favorable position to serve as the "go-betweens" of polity and society. Each in his own way, lawyer and politician respond to the requirements of increasing complexity in the social order generally by further developing their specialized roles. And this fosters their increasing integration into the structure of political authority.

Where social organization is relatively simple and collective decision-making can be handled without particular skills in mediation, arbitration, negotiation, bargaining, compromising, coordinat-

---

[4] Talcott Parsons, "A Sociologist Looks at the Legal Profession," in *Essays in Sociological Theory* (rev. ed.; New York: The Free Press of Glencoe, 1954), p. 374.

ing, and so on, lawyers and politicians function within a restricted sphere. But, as relations are established between large corporations, trade associations, labor unions, and other collectivities as influential centers of power; as the growth of administrative regulatory agencies with wide discretionary powers makes for inclusion of once-private matters in the public sector; and as the range of legislative concerns gives rise to a vast proliferation of laws politicizing and legalizing once-private relationships, the distinction between private and public aspects of social and political life becomes increasingly ambiguous and, in many cases, altogether irrelevant. As a result, not only do the professions of law and politics converge as their members acquire similar skills, but both professions are increasingly integrated into the political system—in different ways, to be sure, but in sufficiently similar fashion to foster professional convergence. Professional convergence in this sense means that, as the two professions become more integrated into the political system, their members find opportunities that facilitate the actual interchange of institutional positions, careers, and professional roles more than is the case with other occupations.

The integration of the professions of law and politics in the structure of political authority provides a general criterion that permits speaking of a particular structural isomorphism. In order to identify the isomorphism, the sought-for characteristics must relate the work of the lawyer and the politician to the integration of these professions in the structure of political authority.

LAW AND POLITICS AS PROFESSIONS

That law is a "profession" in whatever way one wishes to define a profession does not require explicit demonstration. But what of politics as a vocation? Is it not too much to assume that even those who devote all their time to politics are "professionals" in the same sense as that in which lawyers, doctors, or engineers are professionals? The answer is probably that, in empirical reality, it may indeed be too much to assume that politics is a profession like those of law, medicine, or engineering. And the politicians discussed in the empirical analyses of this study are not "professional" in the sense in which the term is conventionally used.

But the interest of this study, it must be re-emphasized, is theoretical, not empirical. Isomorphic analysis does not require that two phenomena have all properties in common, though they obviously must have enough in common to permit comparison. Moreover, as isomorphic theorizing seeks to extend the range of empirical observation, it may be fruitful to look at both law and politics from the standpoint of the sociology of professions. It need not be assumed that politics is *in fact* a full-fledged profession in order to deal with it from this standpoint. Indeed, this perspective may suggest the "professional potential" of politics as a vocation and, as a result, serve as a yardstick in prognosticating about the future of politics as a vocation. Such prognostication is not the objective here, though a "developmental construct" of politics as a profession may be useful in appraising current manifestations of what may be a long-range trend.

In dealing with both law and politics in the perspective of the sociology of professions, it is not necessary to introduce all the criteria that might be mustered in defining "profession," but only those which are particularly relevant in explicating the professional convergence of law and politics. Three criteria, then, will be used to assess the professional status of each field—the presumed "independence" of the professional worker in contrast to other occupational types; the more or less explicit articulation of a set of norms that are designed to guide the professional's conduct; and the professional's alleged orientation to "service" rather than to private gain.

Professional Independence.   Perhaps more than by anything else, professions are set off from other occupations by the requirement that they be relatively independent of control by laymen who, by definition, do not have the requisite training and skills to judge the work of professionals. Lawyers have, of course, always taken great pride in their independence. The lawyer's independence is assumed to be a necessary condition of his effective performance of the functions that he is called upon to undertake, vis-à-vis both his clients and the institutional structure in which he has, at least traditionally, performed his work—the system of courts. Not the least important criticism periodically made of the legal profession is that it fails to live up to this criterion. As the historian Richard Hofstadter has reported, in the opening decade of the present century,

> . . . with the rise of corporate industrialism and finance capitalism, the law, particularly in the urban centers where the most enviable prices were to be had, was becoming a captive profession.[5]

The charge of the legal profession's captivity by business and financial interests is still common and often appears in a highly vulgar and biased form.[6] Such conspiratorial approaches ignore altogether the fact that the lawyer has also become, to use the invidious term, the "captive" of labor unions[7] and the government bureaucracy.[8] Undoubtedly, the meaning of "independence" has changed; but if the lawyer has become an "organization man," it is all the more important to study rather than condemn the profession's relationship to the organizations in which he performs his functions. As Talcott Parsons has pointed out in a comment on the approach of the late sociologist C. Wright Mills, especially with regard to the *control* processes in the business world:

> Mills tends to assume that the relation between law and business is an overwhelming one-way relation; lawyers are there to serve the

---

[5] Richard Hofstadter, *The Age of Reform* (New York: Alfred A. Knopf, 1955), p. 158.

[6] See, for instance, C. Wright Mills, *White Collar: The American Middle Classes* (New York: Oxford University Press, 1951), pp. 121–129.

[7] For a lucid discussion of the roles played by lawyers in labor unions, see Harold L. Wilensky, *Intellectuals in Labor Unions: Organizational Pressures on Professional Roles* (New York: The Free Press of Glencoe, 1956).

[8] For the lawyer in government, see Albert P. Blaustein and Charles O. Porter, *The American Lawyer: A Summary of the Survey of the Legal Profession* (Chicago: University of Chicago Press, 1954), pp. 58–63.

interests of businessmen and essentially have no independent influence. This, I think, is an illusion stemming largely from Mills'
preoccupation with a certain kind of power. His implicit reasoning
seems to be that since lawyers have less power than businessmen,
they do not really count.[9]

Before the legal profession is indicted *in toto*, it is necessary to be
more specific about the number of lawyers who may be "captive"
and those who presumably are not. In 1958 there were 262,320
lawyers listed in the Martindale-Hubbell census. They were distributed into various categories, as follows:

Private practice	73.0%
Government service	9.0
Salaried in private industry	7.0
Judiciary	3.0
Law school	0.4
Other	7.6
Total	100.0%

These figures do not discriminate between types of private practice.
But of the 176,680 practicing lawyers reported on in the Survey of
the Legal Profession in the early fifties, almost 68 per cent were
individual practitioners having neither partners nor associates; 27
per cent were partners in law firms; and 5 per cent were associates
in law firms.[10]

Clearly, it is hazardous to generalize to the legal profession as a
whole, especially in a study of lawyers in politics. If, in the analyses,
lawyers were treated as a single group, it was because more refined
categories would have made quantitative analysis impossible. Nevertheless, in view of the fact that most lawyer-legislators are private

---

[9] Talcott Parsons, "The Distribution of Power in American Society," in
Structure and Process in Modern Societies (New York: The Free Press of Glencoe, 1960), p. 219.

[10] Blaustein and Porter, *op. cit.*, p. 8.

practitioners, it can be assumed that they are reasonably independent.

But does the politician meet the standard of independence in such a way that one can meaningfully speak of politics as a profession? The question is admittedly complex, and an answer must necessarily be conditional. In one respect—the institutional—the politician cannot be considered "independent" at all. As an elected public official, he is dependent on the electorate, just as the lawyer is dependent on clients who may or may not come to his office. Of course, some elective officials have, under certain conditions, achieved a great deal of independence from their constituents—partly by virtue of lack of competition for the office they occupy, or partly because their personal stature as statesmen makes their re-election almost automatic. But this kind of independence is seen more appropriately as an attribute of particular individuals than as an attribute of the political profession.

Yet, as the perennial controversy over the "nature" of representation shows, the politician's status vis-à-vis his nominal "superiors" has always been ambiguous. Should his representative role be that of a "free agent" unbound by a mandate, or that of a "delegate" who must follow instructions from his various clienteles?[11] Once the distinction between institutional status and political role is made, the politician, though clearly dependent on the electorate for his status as an officeholder, may yet be independent in his relations with his clients. In other words, the politician's client relationship is very much like that of the lawyer, who is "retained" by his client— that is, dependent on the client for employment, yet independent in regard to the roles he may take in the relationship.

Empirical evidence in recent studies about legislator-client relations indicates that the politician's representational style is structurally isomorphic with the lawyer's style. The reasons for this are

---

[11] See Heinz Eulau, John C. Wahlke, William Buchanan, and LeRoy C. Ferguson, "The Role of the Representative: Some Empirical Observations on the Theory of Edmund Burke," *American Political Science Review*, LIII (September 1959), 742–756.

many, but two may be mentioned. First, unable to give instructions in an ever more complex society, the political client must increasingly depend on the representative for correct decisions on the basis of his own appraisal of the problem at hand. Reciprocally, representatives find it increasingly difficult to consult their clients because electoral districts have grown in size and heterogeneity of population. Under these conditions, the politician tends to become increasingly independent in his client relations. In this sense, then, the politician can meet or approximate the independence criterion set for the professional. And the trend toward increasing independence in politician–client role relations is likely to be accentuated in the future, contributing to the professionalization of politics as a vocation.

Professional Ethics. Its independence from direct supervision by laymen as well as by political authority places a profession in a position where the improper use of its special skills and competences could easily do enormous social harm. In particular, the exploitation and manipulation of clients for personal gain or advantage would not seem out of the question. In order to protect both the profession's clients and its own reputation and prestige, and to safeguard the profession's position of trust in the community, most professions have developed more or less explicit codes of ethics or appropriate etiquette directed toward the self-regulation of relations with peers, clients, and society in general. The specific norms of conduct of a profession are, therefore, a second criterion by which its "professionalism" can be appraised. Responsible professional behavior can be judged in terms of the professional's adherence to the code of professional ethics.

The distinctive aspect of professional ethics is not the fact that it provides standards of proper conduct; it is the formalization of these standards in the code itself. In general, most codes of professional ethics are not unique but represent the application of generally accepted ethical rules of behavior to the particular spheres of the profession's competence. The lawyer, for instance, is seen as subject to very specific duties to his clients, the public, his professional colleagues, and himself. As a result of such multiple commitments, lawyers may at times experience serious conflicts concerning appropriate conduct. Should the lawyer lie for his client? Should he defend an accused person if he is convinced of the person's guilt? What is and what is not "conflict of interest"? How can the lawyer make himself known without advertising his business? There is disagreement within the legal profession concerning these and other questions of proper professional conduct. But the fact that the matter is discussed, time and again, is enough proof of the profession's sensitivity to the importance of its code of ethics as a safeguard of its professional status.

The politician's status as a professional from this perspective again presents a more difficult problem. For a long time it was assumed that politics was guided by a peculiar code, however informal, that freed the politician from conformity with ordinary ethical standards. But there cannot be permanent conflict between politics and ethics, because a code of professional political ethics, if such were to be written, could not avoid incorporating and applying the principles that belong to social ethics generally. An ethics that did not meet generally accepted standards of behavior would make politics a deviant profession, indeed—a situation that is most unlikely.

Though the condition may derive from public ignorance and from a traditional lack of respect for authority, politics remains a "dirty word" in the United States.[12] The history of American politics, if it were to be a very partial history, could be written as the history of corruption. As Hyman and Sheatsley have noted in commenting on the public opinion polls concerning politics as a vocation, many people

> . . . took the stand that it was "almost impossible" for a man to go into politics without becoming dishonest. This same reason, incidentally, was advanced by about half of the group who would not like to see their sons enter politics: public service is essentially dishonest and corrupting. Many among those who would favor a political career

---

[12] Maurice Klain, "Politics—Still a Dirty Word," *Antioch Review*, XV (December 1955), 457–466.

for their sons explain their attitude by saying that politics is corrupt now and honest men are needed to reform it. Yet, when asked whether or not they are satisfied with the way most office holders in their state are handling their jobs, about half the population indicate satisfaction.[13]

The status of the politician is ambivalent. As William C. Mitchell has pointed out in a perceptive attempt at explanation, the fact that

Americans have tended to regard political offices as not requiring any special training and the fact that political office has been so accessible to the poor and formally uneducated has in turn attracted persons whose performances in office have not always been very exemplary. Thus, a vicious circle developed in which offices with low status attracted less desirable office-holders and their inadequate or corrupt actions further confirmed the low status of public office.[14]

The condition described here is probably no longer valid, and insofar as it was valid it was so largely on the "lower" levels of politics and mainly in the great urban centers. It does, however, help in explaining the traditional view as it seems to have been historically determined. The fact that there is no code of ethics for politicians would seem to confirm popular apprehensions.

This is not to deny that the development of a voluntary code of ethics for politicians presents difficulties that may be *sui generis*. What is and what is not permissible conduct in politics is likely to be more ambiguous than in other areas of social life precisely because politics, by definition, operates in a twilight zone of behavior where disagreement over acts of omission and commission makes the problem of sanctions in the case of breakage of norms particularly

---

[13] Herbert H. Hyman and Paul B. Sheatsley, "The Current Status of American Public Opinion," in John C. Payne (ed.), *The Teaching of Contemporary Affairs* (Menasha, Wisc.: George Banta Publishing Company, 1951), p. 22.

[14] William C. Mitchell, "The Ambivalent Social Status of the American Politician," *Western Political Quarterly*, XII (September 1959), 696. In the National Opinion Research Center survey of occupations, state governor ranked second; federal cabinet member, fourth; mayor of large city, sixth; congressman, seventh; and head of department in state government, twelfth. See Albert J. Reiss, Jr., *Occupations and Social Status* (New York: The Free Press of Glencoe, 1961), p. 54, Table II-9.

subtle,[15] and where the relationship between means and ends is always a matter of continuing formulation rather than of definitive settlement. But efforts to establish codes of ethics for both the executive and legislative branches of government, often including prohibitions that already have legal sanction, suggest that politics is not immune to this aspect of professionalization.[16]

Perhaps more telling than these formal attempts to bring norms of professional ethical conduct to politics is the discovery that there exist, in fact, numerous informal rules of behavior—often called "rules of the game" and sometimes "folkways"—that are more or less specific concerning what is and what is not proper political behavior. Particularly in legislative bodies, as recent research, including this study, shows, there can be found many unwritten and even unspoken norms whose influence on conduct must not be underestimated. Moreover, all indications are that these "rules of the game" are viewed as being of great functional value to political success.[17] Just why these rules of the political game have not as yet been formalized in a code is an interesting question. It is well to point out, therefore, that, except in the case of a few professions, professional codes of ethics do not antedate 1900, and the great majority of them have been adopted since 1918.[18] It would seem

---

[15] See Harry W. Jones, "Political Behavior and the Problem of Sanctions," in Harold D. Lasswell and Harlan Cleveland (eds.), *The Ethic of Power: The Interplay of Religion, Philosophy, and Politics* (New York: Harper & Brothers, 1962), pp. 193–207.

[16] See Wayne A. R. Leys, "A Comparative Investigation of the Norms of Official Conduct," in Harlan Cleveland and Harold D. Lasswell (eds.), *Ethics and Bigness: Scientific, Academic, Religious, Political, and Military* (New York: Harper & Brothers, 1962), pp. 3–19.

[17] See John C. Wahlke, Heinz Eulau, William Buchanan, and LeRoy C. Ferguson, *The Legislative System: Explorations in Legislative Behavior* (New York: John Wiley & Sons, 1962), pp. 141–169: "The Rules of the Game." See also Donald R. Matthews, "The Folkways of the Senate," in *U.S. Senators and Their World* (Chapel Hill: University of North Carolina Press, 1960), pp. 92–117.

[18] See Benson Y. Landis (ed.), "Ethical Standards and Professional Conduct," *The Annals of the American Academy of Political and Social Science*, CCXCVII (January 1955), for discussion of codes of ethics in such professions as accounting, architecture, medicine, law, engineering, ministry, teaching, and public administration.

that, even though a professional ethics of politics is underdeveloped, there is enough consensus among politicians as to what is proper conduct in office to suggest that, from this point of view, politics may partake of more professionalism than is often assumed.

Professional Service. Closely linked to the standard of independence in a profession's definition, and often explicitly incorporated in its code of ethics, is the criterion of public service. In their own judgment as well as in the estimation of the public, the members of a profession are expected to devote themselves to their occupation as a public responsibility that stems from their monopoly of skills that are highly valued because they are so rare. Possession of these skills and ability to render requisite services is considered a public trust; and—contrary to the general view in the case of ordinary occupations—pecuniary acquisition is not looked upon as a professional's legitimate goal.

In spite of deviations from this ideal, a sense of public responsibility has characterized the moral and intellectual tradition of the legal profession. In the Anglo-American context, this tradition can be traced back to the barristers in the Inns of Court in London during the twelfth and thirteenth centuries. Sons of well-to-do parents, these legal ancestors of the modern lawyer, according to Henry S. Drinker,

> . . . did not have to worry about earning their keep and [they] traditionally looked down on all forms of trade and on the competitive spirit characteristic thereof. They regarded the law in the same way that they did a seat in Parliament—as a form of public service in which the gaining of a livelihood was not an objective. The profession of law hence acquired a certain dignity which it has been the aim of the bar to preserve ever since.[19]

In fact, of course, the ideal is at times violated, and much of the criticism of the lawyer has been directed at his failure to live up to the ideal of service. "His constant need to propagandize himself and his client," writes Otto Kirchheimer, "his putting his talents

---

[19] Henry S. Drinker, in *ibid.*, p. 37.

out for hire to an everchanging clientele, and the aleatory character of his success have brought him along with admiration much criticism and contempt."[20] Nevertheless, the conception that he is not only his client's agent but also an "officer of the court"—a public servant—remains an explicit criterion of the lawyer's professional status. Speaking of the legal profession in particular, Talcott Parsons writes:

> Its members are trained in and integrated with, a distinctive part of our cultural tradition, having a fiduciary responsibility for its maintenance, development and implementation. They are expected to provide a "service" to the public within limits without regard to immediate self-interest. The lawyer has a position of independent responsibility so that he is neither a servant only of the client though he represents his interest, nor of *any* other group, in the lawyer's case, of public authority.[21]

It is probably accurate to say that the lawyer's participation in public affairs is so widely expected because, *as a lawyer*, he is expected, more than any other professional, to devote himself to public service.

The politician is, of course, a public servant by definition. Though his motives are often distrusted, the politician, as Max Weber suggested, in addition to enjoying the possession of power, is conscious that "his life has meaning in the service of a cause."[22] Whatever his private motives, service is, so to speak, "built in" the role of the politician. His often self-declared devotion to "public service" may be a stereotypic conception of his role, but his very survival as a politician is predicated on his fulfillment of the expectations of a public that sees him as a public servant. What are sometimes called his "errand-boy" functions may not rank high in his own estimation, and he may well view them as a nuisance that interferes with his

---

20 Otto Kirchheimer, *Political Justice: The Use of Legal Procedure for Political Ends* (Princeton: Princeton University Press, 1961), p. 242.

21 Parsons, "A Sociologist Looks at the Legal Profession," in *op. cit.*, p. 381.

22 Max Weber, "Politics as a Vocation," in H. H. Gerth and C. Wright Mills (eds.), *From Max Weber: Essays in Sociology* (New York: Oxford University Press, 1946), p. 84.

more lofty functions as a decision-maker. But, insofar as successful performance of these service functions contributes to his survival as an elected public official, they have come to be regarded as the mark of the political "professional" perhaps more than any other aspect of the politician's complex role.

The politician's orientation to public service would not seem to implicate him as much in professional conduct as the professional with a "private" occupation: The politician's performance of service does not seem to be entirely voluntary. Rather, it would seem to be in response to sanctions that can be expected to be enforced in case of lack of service. In other words, public service in the politician's case does not seem to be a corollary of a professional role but rather a corollary of the institutional position that he happens to occupy. The distinction is more sharp in its abstract conceptualization than it probably is in reality. The lawyer, in serving his client, also serves the public precisely because he does not embrace his client's cause. In this sense, then, the lawyer's public service is as inadvertent as that of the politician, a corollary of his "office" rather than of his professional role. In the politician's case, the order may well be reversed: As a public servant he may come to represent, over the long haul or the short, certain special interests whose agent he is in the public arena. But such agency does not seem to detract from the politician's public responsibility unless it leads to forms of conduct that are not tolerable—bribery, corruption, nepotism, and so on —and that are punished by criminal rather than political sanctions.

CONVERGENCE AND THE FUTURE OF LAW AND POLITICS AS PROFESSIONS

This study has identified three convergent characteristics in law and politics that help to define the structural isomorphism of the two professions—professional independence; a code of ethics; and a norm of public service. Convergence in regard to these properties of the two professions seems to be made possible by their integration in the structure of political authority. This integration of the two professions in the structure of authority must not be confused with their affinity, which refers to the fact that lawyers become politicians or politicians choose law as a vocation. As suggested earlier, two phenomena need not come into physical contact with each other or "interact" in empirical reality in order to be considered convergent. It is sufficient that they have the same, or highly similar, forms. Affinity, on the other hand, refers to the empirically demonstrated or demonstrable fact of a close relationship between two phenomena, such as the affinity of law and politics as vocations. Convergence is the conceptual tool through which the affinity of law and politics may be explained. It may be said that lawyers tend to become politicians more than members of other occupations do, or that politicians tend to choose law rather than another career, *because* law and politics are convergent professions.

The notion of professional convergence makes it possible to explain, then, why studies of lawyers in politics, including this one, fail to discover significant differences between lawyer- and non-lawyer-politicians in many of the roles that both must take in the public arena. Moreover, even in regard to roles that still differentiate lawyers from others, such as expert and leader roles, it is probable that the professional convergence of law and politics will, in due time, obliterate present differences. The reason for this is quite simple. As occupational groups with private skills and roles similar to those of the lawyer come to be more widely represented in politics —"new" occupations such as real estate, insurance, public relations, union management, and so on—their members will vie successfully with those of the legal profession in filling roles or posts traditionally monopolized by lawyers. For, just as these "new" occupations have come to take on functions in the private sphere long considered the lawyer's specialties, such as preparing deeds or mortgage papers, or dealing with problems arising out of conditional sales or accidents, they are likely to be available for the performance of functions in the public sphere in fields where, until now, the lawyer's skills as a lawyer—such as expertise in legislative investigation, bill drafting, or parliamentary procedure—gave him an advantage.

Convergence, then, has another result as well: The more law and politics converge as professions, the less distinct will be the particular kind of contribution that the lawyer-politician is likely to make to politics as a lawyer. Whether this development will have the effect of displacing the lawyer as the most ubiquitous private-occupational type and of reducing his prominence in positions of leadership is an empirical question that cannot be answered at this time. But one might suggest as a very general hypothesis that, the more politics becomes professionalized, the greater is the probability of further convergence. For, if the two professions are initially convergent, greater professionalism in politics should mean that the two professions will become more similar structurally—that is, that the political behavior of lawyers and politicians will tend to be identical. If this is so, it would be expected that the affinity of law and politics as vocations would also be accentuated. Present data, being cross-sectional rather than longitudinal, do not permit us to test this developmental hypothesis.

APPENDIX ON METHOD

THE DATA

The data were collected by the State Legislative Research Project, a four-man team effort sponsored and subsidized by the Political Behavior Committee of the Social Science Research Council.[1] During the legislative sessions of 1957, interviews were conducted with state legislators in New Jersey, Ohio, Tennessee, and California. The interview, guided by a schedule providing for both closed- and open-ended questions, was designed to take about an hour and a half, but the duration of interviews actually ranged, in a few cases, from half an hour to five hours. The interviews took place at legislators' desks on the floor and in offices, homes, restaurants, and other places, varying with the peculiar institutional characteristics of a given legislature or the peculiar circumstances of legislators.[2]

---

[1] A full report of the Project is John C. Wahlke, Heinz Eulau, William Buchanan, and LeRoy C. Ferguson, *The Legislative System* (New York: John Wiley & Sons, 1962). For a report on the collaborative aspects of the Project, see the same authors' "The Annals of Research: A Case of Collaboration in Comparative Study of Legislative Behavior," *The American Behavioral Scientist*, IV (May 1961), 3–9.

[2] For detailed discussion of interview procedures and experiences, see Wahlke *et al.*, *The Legislative System*, pp. 441–452; for discussion of the ways in which the interview schedule was constructed and pretested, see *ibid.*, pp. 438–441.

Most of the data used in the Project's original report, like most of the data used in this study, came from respondents' answers to the interview questions. Of these questions, apart from those of an obvious census-type character, the following provided the data for the analyses of this study:[3]

8. How did you become interested in politics? For example:

   (a) What is your earliest recollection of being interested in it?
   (b) What other members of your family or close relatives held public or political office before you yourself did?
   (d) Just how did it come about that you became a legislator?
   (e) Do you expect to continue to run for the legislature? Why is that?
   (f) Are there any other government positions—local, state, or federal—that you would like to seek? (If "yes" or "perhaps"):
   (g) What are they?

10. Now, a couple of questions about the job of being a legislator:

   (a) First of all, how would you describe the job of being a legislator—what are the most important things you should do here?
   (b) Are there any important *differences* between what *you* think this job is and the way your constituents see it? (What are they?)

11. We've been told that every legislature has its *unofficial* rules of the game—certain things members must do and things they must not do if they want the respect and cooperation of fellow members.

   (a) What are some of these things—these "rules of the game" —that a member must observe to hold the respect and cooperation of his fellow members?

---

[3] The full interview schedule is reproduced, along with interviewer instructions, in *ibid.*, Appendix 6, pp. 492–504.

14. (a) Is there any particular subject or field of legislation in which you consider yourself particularly expert—I mean when it comes to dealing with proposed legislation in that field? (What is that?)

(b) Why is that?

In addition, a number of closed questions, calling for "agree-disagree" responses, were used to construct various indexes and other measures that will be described below. All the anecdotal material comes from interviews *with lawyers only* and not with other legislators, except for some statements made by nonlawyer-legislators about lawyers.

A few words might be said here about some of the implications of open-ended questions in a study like this. Some aspects refer to connected statistical problems and will be treated below. Here it is important to point out that the open-ended character of the questions makes it mandatory to consider some of the results as suggestive rather than definitive. Open-ended questions have the advantages of leading to spontaneous and widely ranging responses and of allowing the respondent himself to formulate or "structure" the topic under investigation. But there are certain drawbacks that limit the usefulness of open-ended questions for systematic treatment. In the first place, many respondents gave an answer that could be coded in several analytic categories, thus not permitting the assignment of priorities within a particular response pattern. Second, the respondents differed a great deal in a number of personal characteristics of consequence in answering open-ended questions. A few were suspicious of the interview and gave minimum, if not evasive, answers. Others were more candid. Some were genuinely pressed for time and failed to elaborate as fully as those who were willing to devote a great deal of time to the interview. Still others—especially nonlawyers with relatively little education—were unable to articulate answers to questions about which they had evidently thought little prior to the interview. Fluctuations in mood, in attitude toward the interview (and possibly the interviewer), in verbal facility, or in

self-consciousness about being interviewed lent considerable varia-
bility to the answer patterns.[4]

THE TOOLS

The main tools used in this study, as in the original research, are certain typologies of legislative roles, derived mainly from the open-
ended interview questions, as well as a number of scales built from
closed items in the interview schedule. Though meaningful reading
of the analyses requires some familiarity with the ways in which
these tools were developed, no detailed discussion of them is needed,
and we shall describe them only briefly, directing the interested
reader to the main report of the project wherever it seems feasible
to do so.[5]

Role Typologies

What were called the "purposive," "representational," and "areal"
roles were constructed largely from responses to Question 10, above.
The manifest content of each answer pattern was originally coded in
one or more of the following five categories: characterization of the
job of legislator; objectives of the job; criteria used in decision-
making; lawmaking functions; and non-lawmaking functions. In
general, purposive roles were derived mainly from answers charac-
terizing the job, representational roles from responses concerning
criteria of decision-making, and areal roles from statements about
objectives of the job. However, because of the open-ended nature of
the questions, not all respondents could be assigned to each of the
different role sets. "Pressure-group roles" were constructed somewhat differently, as described on the following pages.

---

[4] For a discussion of answers to open-ended questions and the ways in which
they were coded, see *ibid.*, pp. 454–455.

[5] For a discussion of the construction of role typologies and scales, see *ibid.*,
Appendixes 1 and 2, pp. 465–475.

1. PURPOSIVE ROLE SET[6]

   Tribune: The respondent characterizes his job as "finding out" or "knowing the will of the people"; representing their concerns or expressing their needs and demands. The job should be one of public trust that benefits the people, of protecting or defending the interests of people.

   Inventor: The respondent characterizes the job as "solving problems"; he sees it as having the objective of either promoting the "general welfare" or fostering "better government," or achieving specific policies.

   Broker: The respondent characterizes the job as balancing of conflicting demands and interests, in general as well as between constituents and state or groups, between groups, or between state and groups. The legislator should "see all sides," have an "over-all picture."

2. REPRESENTATIONAL ROLE SET

   Trustee: The respondent says he makes decisions on the basis of conscience (principles), or on the basis of his own judgment and understanding of "facts" or appraisal of interests, and so on.

   Delegate: The respondent claims to make decisions on the basis of instructions from constituents, interest groups, or party.

   Politico: The respondent says that he makes his decisions by weighing his own conscience and/or judgment against instructions; or he claims that, depending on the situation, he will do either one or the other.

3. AREAL ROLE SET

   District-oriented: The respondent sees as the objectives of the job advancing the interests of his district or, in the case of conflict, promoting those of his district *above* those of the state.

   State-oriented: The respondent sees as the objective of his job promoting the interests of the state, and he places these interests *above* those of his district.

---

[6] Two roles in this set, that of Ritualist and that of Opportunist, have not been used in this study and need not be described here.

District–state-oriented: The respondent equates the interests of state and district, sees no conflict, and claims to promote both.

4. PRESSURE-GROUP ROLE SET

The roles in this set were constructed inferentially by combining a measure of legislators' attitudes of friendliness or hostility toward pressure-group activity and a measure of their knowledge or awareness of pressure-group activity. The rationale involved in the construction of these roles has been articulated as follows:

> Legislators can be expected to facilitate or to resist the accommodation of group demands according to their relative friendliness or hostility to pressure-group activity. But it seems obvious that the effectiveness of their actions in either facilitating or resisting such demands will also depend upon their knowledge of the actual character of groups and their demands. Behavior which consistently either facilitates or resists group influence in legislative policy-making requires at least some minimal knowledge about the world of pressure groups. The uninformed legislator's behavior is likely to be erratic and inconsistent in this respect. Similarly, the legislator who is neutral toward pressure-group activity and influence in general cannot be expected to behave in any very consistent manner either.[7]

Attitudes of friendliness or hostility were ascertained by a four-item, Likert-type scale based on responses to the following questions:

1. Would you say that, on the whole, the legislature would work much better, somewhat better, about the same, somewhat worse, or much worse, if there were no interest groups and lobbies trying to influence legislation?
2. The job of the legislator is to work out compromises among conflicting interests. (Do you agree? disagree?)
3. Lobbyists and special interests have entirely too much influence in American state legislatures. (Do you agree? disagree?)

---

[7] Wahlke *et al.*, *The Legislative System*, pp. 469–470.

4. Under our form of government, every individual should take an interest in government directly, not through interest-group organizations. (Do you agree? disagree?)

The reliability of the scale has been described elsewhere, as has been the measure used to determine the degree of awareness of lobbying activity.[8] For the purposes of the latter, respondents were asked to identify the names of a number of lobbyists then more or less active in the respective state legislatures. Cross-tabulation of the two measures—of attitudes of friendliness-hostility and of awareness—yielded the following three role types:

Facilitator: The respondent has a friendly attitude toward group activity *and* relatively much knowledge about it.

Resister: The respondent is hostile toward group activity *and* has relatively much knowledge about it.

Neutral: The respondent has no strong attitude of favor or disfavor to pressure-group activity (regardless of the level of his knowledge), or he has very little knowledge about it (regardless of his hostility or friendliness).

Ideology Scale

This is a three-item Guttman-type scale constructed by Ford's method, using the counter-sorter.[9] The scale is formally and substantively weak—the former, because it consists of only three items altogether; the latter, because it combines an item of a "political" content (civil liberties) with two items of an "economic" content. However, the three items made for a scale with a coefficient of reproducibility of .924, with individual errors well within the acceptable range. It proved its usefulness in the original study by sharply discriminating between Democrats and Republicans in all four states. The scale items are:

---

[8] See *ibid.,* pp. 468–469; see also "American State Legislators' Role Orientations Toward Pressure Groups," *Journal of Politics,* XXII (May 1960), 213–215.

[9] For more detailed discussion, see Wahlke *et al., The Legislative System,* p. 475.

1. The government has the responsibility to see to it that all people, poor or rich, have adequate housing, education, medical care, and protection against unemployment. (Do you agree? disagree?)
2. Business enterprise can continue to give us our high standard of living only if it remains free from government regulation. (Do you agree? disagree?)
3. A man whose loyalty has been questioned before a legislative committee, but who swears under oath that he has never been a Communist, should be permitted to teach in our public schools. (Do you agree? disagree?)

Partisanship Scale

This is a four-item Guttman-type scale with an over-all coefficient of reproducibility of .908. "Disagree" answers to items 1 and 2, and "agree" answers to items 3 and 4, were considered pro-party responses. The scale items are:

1. The best interests of the people would be better served if legislators were elected without party labels.
2. Under our form of government, every legislator should take an interest in government directly, not through a political party.
3. If a bill is important for his party's record, a member should vote with his party even if it costs him some support in his district.
4. The two parties should take clear-cut, opposing stands on more of the important state issues in order to encourage party responsibility.

THE SAMPLE AND STATISTICAL PROBLEMS

The original project hoped to interview the entire population or universe of persons who, in 1957, were members of the four legislatures. This goal was achieved for all practical purposes—with 100 per cent of the legislators being interviewed in New Jersey, 94 per cent in both Ohio and California, and 91 per cent in Tennessee. For this reason, if for no other, the problem of statistical inference from a population sample to a population universe would not seem to be relevant.

Of course, combining the data from the four states would constitute a "sample" of some larger universe—admittedly an ill-defined universe, for it might be all state legislators sitting in 1957, or all legislators on whatever level, or all legislators past, present, and future. But no such assumption is warranted, and combining the data from the four states (as, indeed, was done in other substudies of the project), would present a "sample" of a most dubious kind.[10] Therefore, combined totals for the four states were not presented in this study as they might well have been if the study dealt with random probability samples rather than with institutional universes.

But this does not exhaust all that must be said about the statistical aspects of the data. In the first place, even though the data seem to be dealing with four self-contained universes, there is the problem of the statistical significance of data derived from open-ended questions. Open-ended questions do not permit the making of categorical statements about our universes that might be made if only direct, closed questions were asked; for open-ended questions make for a great many answer patterns that, within an analytical category, are really "non-responses." For example, the fact that a certain proportion of respondents might mention their occupational background as reason for their considering themselves "experts" in particular fields of legislation does not mean that others, who did not mention this, were unaffected by their occupation, and that, had they been asked a direct question, they would not have referred to their occupation in explaining their self-declared expertise.

In other words, the data often actually deal with a "sample" rather than with the universe, but the interviewer has no "say" in selecting the sample. The fact that some interviewees would and others would not refer to some aspect of a possible answer rather than to

---

[10] This and other statistical problems connected with the study of institutional populations are discussed more fully in *ibid.*, pp. 455–463.

some other aspect makes these respondents anything but a random sample. To put this a bit differently, it cannot be said, in the case of responses to open-ended questions, whether the "not ascertained" responses were due to chance. Rather, it must be assumed that they were not due to chance—that some aspect of a theoretically "complete" answer was more salient to some than to other respondents. The discovery of such salience is, as has been pointed out, one of the substantive advantages of unstructured, open-ended questions. But it is disturbing from a statistical point of view.

In addition to "non-response bias," there are other problems of a quasi-statistical sort, such as random errors other than sampling errors, and the problem of *ex post facto* hypotheses. A few words should be said here about the latter. Although these analyses were undertaken with theoretical notions in mind, specific hypotheses for testing were not formulated in advance. In survey research, even if there be *a priori* hypotheses, they are likely to be modified once initial tabulations are examined. As a result of such inspection, further hypotheses are *derived* from the data. But if hypotheses are adjusted in this way or newly proposed after the data have been looked at, it is certainly illegitimate to test such *post facto* propositions for statistical significance. For this procedure is circular and gives a purely spurious impression of "proof." It might be added that, even in studies based on probability samples, the "hard" but also narrow notion that one need apply *only* tests of statistical significance in order to make meaningful statements has been increasingly rejected by social scientists, for two reasons—first, what is statistically not significant may yet be theoretically interesting or socially important; and, second, negative findings may be as "telling" as positive ones: The "deviant case" may serve as a source of speculation about the validity of a hypothesis as much as the case that conforms to theoretical expectations.

One final point: As any sophisticated reader will readily discover, in analyzing the data the occupational factor has not been "controlled" by other factors. For instance, it might have been desirable to control lawyer- and nonlawyer-legislators' responses to a variety of questions by their age, length of service, education, status mobility, and so on—all factors that, in one way or another, might affect responses. In other words, some of the reported "findings" may be spurious. Yet, the analyst takes the risk of assuming that they are not. The reason for not introducing obvious controls is a simple one. Given the fact that in many columns the number of "not ascertained" responses is large, reducing the size of lawyer and non-lawyer populations (which are not large in the first place) and further subdividing the groups through controlling them would have reduced the number of cases in many cells of a table to such an extent that the percentage distributions would be even more unstable than they are already.

A NOTE ON THE MEANING OF COMPARISON

In the absence of statistical tests of significance, it is yet necessary to have some other standard by which to evaluate the numerical distributions. We feel that similarities or differences in *patterns* of distributions from one state to another may be used for this purpose. Although the comparative method is a general strategy of inquiry, we propose to use it here as a *technique* and as a viable substitute for statistical analysis.

Fruitful application of the comparative method to individual data for the purpose of molar analysis—as when we speak of lawyers and nonlawyers as aggregates, or of lawyers as a group in one state as against lawyers as a group in another state—is predicated on a number of requirements that must be met in order to make possible valid inferences from the evidence that is being compared. We need not spell out all these requirements in detail, especially those of a technical sort—important as they are. We are satisfied that these requirements were met as well in the original project as they have ever been met in comparative political research.[11]

---

[11] For further discussion of problems of comparative method, see Heinz Eulau, "A Note on Comparative Analysis," *Midwest Journal of Political Science*, VI (November 1962), 397–407.

To achieve its objectives, comparative analysis must be conducted in a theoretical framework that is flexible enough not to do violence to variations in the empirical data, especially those variations which are due to different institutional parameters; yet this framework must also be sufficiently unified and abstract in order to accommodate these variations. The theoretical framework, then, provides that *tertium comparationis* without which comparison is impossible. It has, of course, other functions as well, but it supplies a standard that is not itself empirical, and that can be used to appraise the meaning of patterns in the distribution of the data that are to be compared. If these patterns are consistent, a criterion for judging the validity of inferences is available. In our statements about lawyer- and nonlawyer-legislators, we rely heavily on the presence or absence of expected patterns from one state to the next as criteria of discrimination.

Second, the categories of analysis must be functional rather than conventional. In other words, unless functional concepts are used— concepts that refer to behavioral equivalences rather than to structural features that may *seem* to be, but are not, behaviorally equivalent—comparison may result in attempts to compare phenomena that cannot or should not be compared. Much of the global analysis most often used in the comparative study of aggregates or institutions is not really comparative, though it may seem so, because the language of aggregate and institutional analysis conceals a good deal of the variances in behavior that the use of individual data reveals. The harnessing of these variances, however, requires functional categories of analysis, such as the role typologies used in this study.

Third, comparative analysis of patterns as a technique permits us to overcome the numerical paucity of the individual data, which makes introduction of appropriate controls difficult. By dealing with responses in four different institutional contexts, we are, in fact, controlling the individual data by their institutional parameters. These parameters provide interpretative criteria for "explaining" outcomes that seem to defy theoretical expectations. For instance, the relative "youth" of California as a state—compared with the other three states of this study—is likely to be an independent factor that affects the career origins and career lines of politicians. Or the low legislative pay in Tennessee is likely to affect legislators' career aspirations.

These "institutional" factors cannot be expressed in a rigorous, quantitative way, but not to use such institutional knowledge in the analysis of behavioral data would be rather ludicrous. The failure of behavioral data within a given institutional setting, compared with other settings, to meet theoretical expectations may, in fact, aid in interpretation. In this respect, then, comparative analysis is equivalent to replication in experimental research—as if a number of experiments had been conducted. It suggests that the "deviant case" is perhaps "unique" not because of some "essential" or "intrinsic" property it may possess, but because it deviates from what one might theoretically expect and from what, in fact, one finds empirically in most other cases. For this reason we did not hesitate to invoke "institutional explanations" in analyses where institutional parameters clearly affect the results of behavioral findings.

INDEX